Cooking Light.

POULTRY

Cooking Light®

POULTRY

80 Delectable and Nutritious, and Very Different
Recipes for Chicken, Turkey, and Cornish Hen

WARNER BOOKS

A Time Warner Company

PHOTOGRAPHER: *Jim Bathie*

PHOTO STYLIST: *Kay E. Clarke*

BOOK DESIGN: *Giorgetta Bell McRee*

COVER DESIGN: *Andrew Newman*

Warner Books, Inc., 666 Fifth Avenue, New York, NY 10103

A Time Warner Company

Printed in the United States of America
First printing: February 1991
10 9 8 7 6 5 4 3 2

Library of Congress Cataloging-in-Publication Data

Cooking light poultry.
    p.   cm.—(Cooking light)
  Includes index.
  ISBN 0–446–39183–2
  1. Cookery (Poultry) I. Title: Poultry. II. Series: Cooking
light (New York, N.Y.)
TX750.C66 1991
641.6'65—dc20   90–12859
                                             CIP

CONTENTS

EATING WELL IS THE BEST REWARD

Welcome to **Cooking Light**, a cookbook that celebrates the pleasures of good health. These low-fat, low-calorie recipes are easy to make, a delight to behold, and a feast for the senses.

Guided by the belief that good health and good food are synonymous, **Cooking Light** provides an approach to eating and cooking that is both healthy and appealing. Using the eighty recipes in this book, you will see how easy it is to minimize fat and sodium while maximizing minerals, fiber, and vitamins. And you will be delighted by the emphasis on the good taste and texture of fresh wholesome food cooked the light way.

So eat hearty, slim down and delight yourself, your family, and your friends with these easy-to-prepare, all-natural, and very delicious recipes.

EDITOR'S NOTE

Unless otherwise indicated:

eggs are large

margarine is corn oil margarine

sugar is granulated white sugar

flour is all-purpose

raisins are "dark"

cranberries and other ingredients are fresh

prepared mustard is regular store-bought yellow mustard

chicken breast is cooked without skin and without salt

vinegar is regular distilled vinegar

Cooking Light.

POULTRY

COLD DISHES

CHICKEN PÂTÉ

1½ cups finely chopped cooked chicken breast
½ (8-ounce) package Neufchâtel cheese, softened
3 tablespoons chopped onion
2 tablespoons dry sherry
2 tablespoons reduced-calorie mayonnaise
2 teaspoons lemon juice
¼ teaspoon hot sauce
⅛ teaspoon ground nutmeg
Vegetable cooking spray
Paprika
Fresh parsley sprigs (optional)

Combine chicken, Neufchâtel, onion, sherry, mayonnaise, lemon juice, hot sauce, and nutmeg in container of an electric blender; process until smooth. Transfer mixture to a 2-cup mold coated with cooking spray. Cover mixture, and chill overnight.

Unmold onto a serving plate; sprinkle with paprika. Garnish with parsley sprigs, if desired. Serve with melba toast rounds or unsalted crackers. Yield: 1¾ cups (28 calories per tablespoon).

PROTEIN 2.8 / FAT 1.5 / CARBOHYDRATE 0.3 / FIBER 0.0 / CHOLESTEROL 10 / SODIUM 30 / POTASSIUM 27

LIGHT CHICKEN TERRINE

1 medium-size sweet red pepper, seeded and chopped
1 medium-size green pepper, seeded and chopped
¾ cup diced carrot
½ cup diced onion
1¼ pounds boneless chicken breasts, skinned
1 teaspoon chicken-flavored bouillon granules
½ teaspoon white pepper
½ teaspoon curry powder
½ teaspoon hot sauce
1 (13-ounce) can evaporated skim milk, divided
¼ cup dry white wine
1 egg
1 egg white
1 medium bunch romaine lettuce
Vegetable cooking spray
Carrot curls (optional)

Steam peppers, carrot, and onion in a vegetable steamer over boiling water 10 minutes. Drain well on paper towels. Set aside.

Cut chicken into 1-inch pieces; set aside. Position knife blade in bowl of food processor; add bouillon granules, white pepper, curry powder, hot sauce, and half of prepared chicken. Process 1½ minutes or until smooth, scraping bowl once. Remove food pusher. Slowly pour ¾ cup evaporated skim milk, wine, and egg through food chute with the processor running, blending just until smooth. Spoon mixture into a large bowl. Repeat procedure with remaining chicken, evaporated skim milk, and egg white. Stir chicken mixtures together.

Coat bottom and sides of an 8½- x 4½- x 3-inch loaf pan with cooking spray. Line bottom and sides of loaf pan with romaine leaves, dull side up. Allow leaves to hang over sides of pan. Spread half of chicken mixture in bottom and two-thirds up sides of pan. Spoon prepared vegetables over center well of chicken mixture. Spread remaining chicken mixture over vegetables.

Cover pan tightly with aluminum foil; punch a hole in foil to allow steam to escape. Place loaf pan in a 13- x 9- x 2-inch baking pan.

Fill baking pan with hot water to a depth of 1½ inches. Bake at 350° for 1 hour and 15 minutes or until terrine is firm and center springs back after touching. Remove foil from loaf pan, and allow terrine to cool. When warm to touch, pour off excess liquid. Cool completely. Unmold terrine onto a serving platter; cover with heavy-duty plastic wrap, and refrigerate overnight.

Let stand at room temperature 30 minutes. Slice with an electric knife. Garnish with carrot curls, if desired. Yield: 10 servings (122 calories per serving).

PROTEIN 16.9 / FAT 2.3 / CARBOHYDRATE 6.9 / FIBER 0.5 / CHOLESTEROL 64 / SODIUM 126 / POTASSIUM 345

SMOKED TURKEY PÂTÉ

1½ pounds boneless smoked turkey breast, cut into cubes
½ (8-ounce) package Neufchâtel cheese, softened
3 tablespoons Chablis or other dry white wine
2 teaspoons finely grated onion
¼ teaspoon white pepper
¼ teaspoon celery seeds
⅛ teaspoon ground nutmeg
Vegetable cooking spray
Fresh parsley sprigs (optional)
Pimiento strips (optional)
Olive slice (optional)

Position knife blade in food processor bowl; add first 7 ingredients, and process until smooth. Spoon into a 2½-cup mold coated with cooking spray. Cover and chill overnight.

Unmold onto a serving plate, and garnish with parsley sprigs, if desired. Arrange pimiento strips and olive slice over top of pâté, if desired. Serve with melba toast rounds. Yield: 2½ cups (32 calories per tablespoon).

PROTEIN 4.8 / FAT 1.2 / CARBOHYDRATE 0.1 / FIBER 0.0 / CHOLESTEROL 13 / SODIUM 21 / POTASSIUM 51

COLD GRILLED CHICKEN WITH EXOTIC FRUIT

8 (4-ounce) boneless chicken breast halves, skinned
¾ cup unsweetened pineapple juice
¼ cup reduced-sodium soy sauce
2 tablespoons lime juice
1 clove garlic, minced
8 mesquite chips
Vegetable cooking spray
Blueberry Sauce (recipe follows)
1 medium starfruit, sliced
2 medium kiwi, peeled and sliced
8 medium-size fresh strawberries

Trim excess fat from chicken. Rinse chicken with cold water, and pat dry. Place chicken in a shallow container. Combine pineapple juice, soy sauce, lime juice, and garlic, stirring well. Pour over chicken; cover and marinate in refrigerator 8 hours or overnight, turning occasionally. Drain; reserve marinade.

Cover mesquite chips with water, and soak 30 minutes. Drain chips, and place directly on medium coals. Coat grill with cooking spray. Grill chicken 4 to 5 inches over medium-hot coals 5 minutes on each side or until chicken is tender, basting once with reserved marinade. Remove chicken from grill, and chill thoroughly.

Spoon 2 tablespoons Blueberry Sauce onto 8 individual serving plates. Place each chicken breast half in Blueberry Sauce. Top each serving with 1 slice of starfruit, 2 slices of kiwi, and 1 strawberry. Yield: 8 servings (198 calories per serving).

Blueberry Sauce:

1 cup fresh blueberries
2 tablespoons water
2 tablespoons crème de cassis
1 teaspoon lemon juice

Combine blueberries, water, and crème de cassis in a small saucepan. Bring to a boil; reduce heat, and simmer 1 to 2 minutes.

Remove from heat, and cool. Transfer mixture to container of electric blender or food processor; process until smooth. Stir in lemon juice. Cover and chill thoroughly. Yield: 1 cup.

PROTEIN 27.1 / FAT 3.3 / CARBOHYDRATE 12.9 / CHOLESTEROL 70 / IRON 1.2 / SODIUM 354 / CALCIUM 28

CHILLED CHICKEN WITH DILL SAUCE

8 (4-ounce) boneless chicken breast halves, skinned
½ cup reduced-calorie Italian salad dressing
2 tablespoons water
1 tablespoon lime juice
1 tablespoon white wine vinegar
1 clove garlic, crushed
Vegetable cooking spray
Lime wedges
Dill Sauce (recipe follows)

Trim excess fat from chicken. Place each piece between 2 sheets of waxed paper; flatten to ¼-inch thickness, using a meat mallet or rolling pin. Place chicken in a 13- x 9- x 2-inch baking dish. Combine next 5 ingredients in a small bowl; pour over chicken. Cover and refrigerate 2 hours.

Remove chicken from marinade, discarding marinade. Coat grill with cooking spray. Grill chicken 6 inches over medium coals 8 minutes, turning once.

Arrange chicken on a serving platter; garnish with lime wedges. Serve either warm or chilled with 1½ tablespoons Dill Sauce per serving. Yield: 8 servings (160 calories per serving).

Dill Sauce:

½ cup plain low-fat yogurt
¼ cup low-fat cottage cheese
1½ teaspoons lime juice

1½ teaspoons chopped green onion
½ teaspoon dried whole dillweed
⅛ teaspoon white pepper

Combine all ingredients in container of an electric blender; process until smooth. Cover and chill thoroughly. Yield: 1 cup.

PROTEIN 27.5 / FAT 3.3 / CARBOHYDRATE 3.3 / FIBER 0.0 / CHOLESTEROL 72 / SODIUM 236 / POTASSIUM 264

COLD FRUITED CHICKEN

¼ cup dried apricot halves, quartered
¼ cup chopped red onion
2 tablespoons dry white wine
2 tablespoons unsweetened orange juice
1½ teaspoons red wine vinegar
2 cups chopped, cooked chicken or turkey breast
½ cup coarsely chopped orange segments
½ cup seedless red or green grapes
¼ cup sliced almonds, toasted
¼ cup chopped fresh parsley
¼ teaspoon pepper
⅛ teaspoon salt
Dash of crushed red pepper
4 leaves red leaf lettuce

Combine first 5 ingredients in a saucepan, and bring to a boil. Set aside to cool.

Combine apricot mixture with chicken, orange, grapes, almonds, parsley, pepper, salt, and crushed red pepper in a large bowl; cover and chill 1 to 2 hours. Spoon chicken mixture onto a lettuce-lined platter to serve. Yield: 4 servings (229 calories per serving).

PROTEIN 24.5 / FAT 6.3 / CARBOHYDRATE 19.7 / FIBER 1.7 / CHOLESTEROL 59 / SODIUM 132 / POTASSIUM 616

MAIN DISHES

Chicken

CHICKEN-VEGETABLE POT PIES

2 (6-ounce) skinned chicken breast halves
2½ cups water
2 medium baking potatoes, peeled and cut into ½-inch
  cubes
½ cup chopped celery
1 teaspoon chicken-flavored bouillon granules
1 (10-ounce) package frozen mixed vegetables
2 tablespoons unsalted margarine
2 tablespoons all-purpose flour
1 cup skim milk
1 teaspoon poultry seasoning
1 (4-ounce) can sliced mushrooms, drained
Vegetable cooking spray
1 cup all-purpose flour
1 teaspoon baking powder
¼ teaspoon salt
1 tablespoon plus 1½ teaspoons unsalted margarine
½ cup nonfat buttermilk

Combine chicken and water in a large saucepan. Bring to a boil.
Cover, reduce heat, and simmer 30 minutes or until chicken is
tender. Remove chicken, reserving broth. Bone chicken, and cut
meat into bite-size pieces; set aside.

Add potatoes, celery, and bouillon to broth; bring to a boil.

Cover, reduce heat, and simmer 15 to 20 minutes or until potatoes are tender. Stir in mixed vegetables; set aside.

Melt 2 tablespoons unsalted margarine in a heavy saucepan over low heat; add 2 tablespoons flour, stirring until smooth. Cook 1 minute, stirring constantly. Gradually add skim milk; cook over medium heat, stirring constantly, until mixture is thickened and bubbly. Remove from heat, and stir in poultry seasoning.

Combine reserved chicken, vegetable mixture, white sauce, and mushrooms in a large bowl. Spoon into individual baking dishes that have been coated with cooking spray.

Combine 1 cup flour, baking powder, and salt in a small bowl. Cut in 1 tablespoon plus 1½ teaspoons unsalted margarine with a pastry blender until mixture resembles coarse meal. Stir in buttermilk. Spoon biscuit dough into 6 portions over chicken mixture. Bake at 350° for 1 hour or until biscuits are golden brown. Yield: 6 servings (314 calories per serving).

PROTEIN 18.6 / FAT 8.2 / CARBOHYDRATE 41.0 / CHOLESTEROL 27 / IRON 2.2 / SODIUM 458 / CALCIUM 116

CREAMY CHICKEN POPOVERS

2 cups water
3 (6-ounce) skinned chicken breast halves
1 large carrot, scraped and sliced
1 small onion, sliced
Vegetable cooking spray
1 small onion, chopped
1¼ cups all-purpose flour, divided
¼ teaspoon dried whole tarragon
1¾ cups skim milk, divided
½ cup plain low-fat yogurt
¼ cup Chablis or other dry white wine
½ cup frozen English peas, thawed
2 tablespoons chopped pimiento
¼ teaspoon salt
2 eggs

Combine water, chicken, carrot, and onion in a large saucepan. Bring to a boil; cover, reduce heat, and simmer 30 minutes. Remove chicken from broth; cool. Bone chicken, and cut meat into 1-inch pieces. Set aside. Strain broth, reserving ¾ cup.

Coat a large nonstick skillet with cooking spray; place over medium-high heat until hot. Add onion, and sauté until tender. Gradually add ¼ cup flour and tarragon, stirring well. Gradually stir in ¾ cup skim milk, yogurt, wine, and reserved chicken broth. Cook, stirring constantly, until mixture is thickened and bubbly. Stir in peas, pimiento, and reserved chicken. Set aside, and keep warm.

Combine remaining 1 cup flour and salt, stirring well. Add eggs and remaining 1 cup skim milk; beat with a wire whisk until well blended. Spoon mixture evenly into 6 (6-ounce) custard cups that have been coated with cooking spray. Place 4 inches apart on a baking sheet. Bake at 400° for 45 to 50 minutes or until golden brown. Break open each popover. Spoon ½ cup chicken mixture over each popover. Serve immediately. Yield: 6 servings (276 calories per serving).

PROTEIN 25.4 / FAT 3.9 / CARBOHYDRATE 33.1 / CHOLESTEROL 133 / IRON 2.2 / SODIUM 236 / CALCIUM 162

CURRIED CHICKEN DINNER

2½ cups water
1 cup brown rice, uncooked
1½ teaspoons chicken-flavored bouillon granules
6 (6-ounce) skinned chicken breast halves
2½ cups water
½ teaspoon curry powder
¼ teaspoon salt
2 cups unsweetened orange juice
2 tablespoons cornstarch
2 tablespoons dry sherry
1 teaspoon ground ginger
1 teaspoon grated orange rind
Vegetable cooking spray
2 cups diagonally sliced celery
1 large sweet red pepper, seeded and cut into julienne strips
1 green pepper, seeded and cut into julienne strips

Combine 2½ cups water, rice, and bouillon granules in a medium saucepan; bring to a boil. Cover, reduce heat, and simmer 50 minutes or until liquid is absorbed.

Combine chicken, 2½ cups water, curry powder, and salt in a large Dutch oven; bring to a boil. Cover, reduce heat, and simmer 30 minutes or until chicken is tender; drain. Bone chicken, and cut into bite-size pieces; set meat aside.

Combine orange juice and next 4 ingredients in a small bowl, stirring until cornstarch is dissolved; set aside.

Coat a large nonstick skillet with cooking spray; place over medium-high heat until hot. Add celery and peppers, and sauté until crisp-tender. Stir in reserved chicken and orange juice mixture; bring to a boil. Cook 1 minute, stirring constantly, until thickened. To serve, spoon chicken mixture over hot cooked rice. Yield: 6 servings (332 calories per serving).

PROTEIN 32.1 / FAT 4.5 / CARBOHYDRATE 39.3 / CHOLESTEROL 78 / IRON 2.2 / SODIUM 409 / CALCIUM 51

TROPICAL CHICKEN KABOBS

⅓ cup lime juice
1 tablespoon vegetable oil
1 tablespoon honey
6 (4-ounce) skinned, boned chicken breast halves, cut into 1½-inch pieces
12 pearl onions, peeled
1 large green pepper, seeded and cut into 2-inch pieces
1 papaya, peeled, seeded, and cut into 2-inch pieces
1½ cups fresh pineapple chunks
Vegetable cooking spray

Combine lime juice, vegetable oil, and honey in a shallow dish. Add chicken; toss gently. Cover and marinate in refrigerator 8 hours, stirring occasionally. Remove chicken from marinade, reserving marinade. Alternate chicken, onion, pepper, papaya, and pineapple on 6 (12-inch) skewers. Coat grill rack with cooking spray; place on grill over medium-hot coals. Place kabobs on rack, and cook 15 to 20 minutes or until done, turning and basting frequently with reserved marinade. Yield: 6 servings (222 calories per serving).

PROTEIN 26.6 / FAT 5.7 / CARBOHYDRATE 16.4 / CHOLESTEROL 70 / IRON 1.5 / SODIUM 66 / CALCIUM 36

SPANISH SAFFRON CHICKEN

6 (4-ounce) skinned, boned chicken breast halves
¼ teaspoon freshly ground pepper
Vegetable cooking spray
1 medium onion, sliced
1 clove garlic, minced
½ pound fresh mushrooms, sliced
1 cup water
2 teaspoons paprika
1 teaspoon chicken-flavored bouillon granules
½ teaspoon saffron threads
1 cup frozen English peas
2 tablespoons sliced pitted ripe olives
¼ cup skim milk
1 tablespoon cornstarch
2 tablespoons water
3 cups hot cooked long-grain rice (cooked without salt or
    fat)

Sprinkle chicken with pepper. Place in a large Dutch oven that has been coated with cooking spray. Cook over medium heat until browned.

Wipe pan drippings from Dutch oven with a paper towel. Coat Dutch oven with cooking spray; place over medium-high heat until hot. Add onion, garlic, and mushrooms; sauté until tender. Add chicken, 1 cup water, and next 3 ingredients. Bring to a boil. Cover, reduce heat, and simmer 25 minutes or until chicken is tender. Remove chicken, and set aside.

Add peas, olives, and skim milk to Dutch oven. Cover and simmer 5 minutes. Combine cornstarch and 2 tablespoons water; add to vegetable mixture. Bring to a boil. Reduce heat; cook, stirring constantly, until thickened and bubbly. Remove from heat. To serve, place rice on a serving platter. Arrange chicken over rice; top with vegetable mixture. Yield: 6 servings (335 calories per serving).

PROTEIN 31.2 / FAT 4.4 / CARBOHYDRATE 40.7 / CHOLESTEROL 71 / IRON 3.2 / SODIUM 275 / CALCIUM 56

GRILLED LIME CHICKEN

¼ cup chopped fresh parsley
½ teaspoon freshly ground pepper
½ teaspoon grated lime rind
2 tablespoons lime juice
1 cup Chablis or other dry white wine
6 (4-ounce) skinned, boned chicken breast halves
Vegetable cooking spray
Lime slices (optional)

Combine first 5 ingredients in a shallow baking dish. Add chicken, turning to coat. Cover and marinate in refrigerator 1 hour.

Remove chicken from marinade, reserving marinade. Coat grill rack with cooking spray; place on grill over medium-hot coals. Place chicken on rack, and cook 5 minutes on each side or until done, basting with reserved marinade. Garnish with lime slices, if desired. Yield: 6 servings (146 calories per serving).

PROTEIN 25.8 / FAT 2.9 / CARBOHYDRATE 2.4 / CHOLESTEROL 70 / IRON 1.2 / SODIUM 64 / CALCIUM 21

CRISPY MUSTARD CHICKEN

2 tablespoons reduced-calorie mayonnaise
2 tablespoons prepared mustard
¼ cup wheat germ
⅓ cup fine, dry breadcrumbs
½ teaspoon ground thyme
¼ teaspoon salt
4 (4-ounce) skinned, boned chicken breast halves
Vegetable cooking spray

Combine mayonnaise and mustard in a small bowl; stir well. Combine wheat germ and next 3 ingredients in a shallow bowl. Brush each chicken breast with mustard mixture; dredge in breadcrumb mixture.

Place chicken in a 10- x 6- x 2-inch baking dish that has been coated with cooking spray. Cover and bake at 350° for 40 minutes. Uncover and bake an additional 20 minutes or until chicken is tender. Yield: 4 servings (206 calories per serving).

PROTEIN 29.9 / FAT 5.2 / CARBOHYDRATE 10.0 / CHOLESTEROL 69 / IRON 2.0 / SODIUM 435 / CALCIUM 38

HONEY-BAKED CHICKEN

1 (3-pound) broiler-fryer, skinned
Vegetable cooking spray
¾ cup shredded yellow squash
¾ cup shredded zucchini
½ cup finely chopped onion
½ cup finely chopped celery
1 clove garlic, crushed
1¼ cups toasted whole wheat breadcrumbs
1 egg, beaten
¼ cup chopped pecans
¼ teaspoon salt
¼ teaspoon pepper
3 tablespoons unsweetened apple juice
2 tablespoons honey

Discard giblets and neck of chicken. Rinse chicken under cold, running water, and pat dry. Set aside.

Coat a large nonstick skillet with cooking spray; place over medium-high heat until hot. Add yellow squash, zucchini, onion, celery, and garlic, and sauté until crisp-tender. Drain. Combine vegetable mixture, breadcrumbs, egg, pecans, salt, and pepper in a medium bowl; stir well. Place chicken, breast side up, on a rack in a roasting pan that has been coated with cooking spray. Stuff lightly with dressing mixture. Truss chicken.

Combine apple juice and honey, stirring well. Brush chicken with half of apple juice-honey mixture. Bake at 350° for 1½ to 2 hours or until drumsticks are easy to move and juices run clear, basting occasionally with remaining apple juice-honey mixture. Yield: 6 servings (266 calories per serving).

PROTEIN 26.8 / FAT 10.8 / CARBOHYDRATE 15.6 / CHOLESTEROL 119 / IRON 1.8 / SODIUM 246 / CALCIUM 45

CHINESE CHICKEN-STUFFED PEPPERS

4 large sweet red peppers
Vegetable cooking spray
1 tablespoon sesame oil
1 clove garlic, minced
1 teaspoon minced fresh gingerroot
½ cup finely chopped carrots
¼ cup thinly sliced green onions
1 cup finely chopped, cooked chicken breast (skinned before cooking and cooked without salt)
1 cup cooked regular rice (cooked without salt or fat)
½ cup frozen English peas, thawed and drained
1 egg, beaten
1 tablespoon plus 1½ teaspoons reduced-sodium soy sauce
⅛ teaspoon salt

Cut a ½-inch-thick slice from the side of each pepper, reserving slices; remove seeds. Place peppers in boiling water; boil 5 minutes. Drain and set aside.

Coat a large skillet or wok with cooking spray; add sesame oil, and place over medium heat until hot. Add garlic and gingerroot; stir-fry 30 seconds. Add carrots and green onions; stir-fry 2 minutes. Remove from heat. Add chicken and remaining ingredients, stirring well.

Spoon ¾ cup mixture into each reserved pepper. Top with reserved pepper slices. Arrange peppers, cut side up, in a 10- x 6- x 2-inch baking dish. Cover and bake at 350° for 30 minutes or until thoroughly heated. Yield: 4 servings (231 calories per serving).

PROTEIN 16.4 / FAT 6.7 / CARBOHYDRATE 25.7 / CHOLESTEROL 98 / IRON 3.1 / SODIUM 366 / CALCIUM 37

CHICKEN ÉTOUFFÉE

Vegetable cooking spray
1 large onion, chopped
1 small green pepper, chopped
½ small sweet red pepper, chopped
2 stalks celery, chopped
1 clove garlic, minced
2 tablespoons margarine
2 tablespoons all-purpose flour
3 cups chopped, cooked chicken breast (skinned before cooking and cooked without salt)
¾ cup water
¾ teaspoon chicken-flavored bouillon granules
½ teaspoon dried whole thyme
¼ teaspoon salt
¼ teaspoon red pepper
Dash of hot sauce
2 cups hot cooked parboiled rice (cooked without salt or fat)
1 tablespoon chopped fresh parsley

Coat a large skillet with cooking spray; place over medium heat until hot. Add onion and next 4 ingredients, and sauté until tender. Remove vegetables from skillet; set aside.

Place margarine and flour in large skillet; cook over low heat 5 minutes, stirring constantly, until mixture is the color of a copper penny. Return vegetables to skillet. Add chicken and next 6 ingredients; simmer 2 minutes or until thoroughly heated. Serve over hot cooked rice. Sprinkle with parsley. Yield: 8 servings (182 calories per serving).

PROTEIN 18.0 / FAT 5.0 / CARBOHYDRATE 15.0 / CHOLESTEROL 45 / IRON 1.5 / SODIUM 352 / CALCIUM 32

CRISPY DRUMSTICKS

8 chicken drumsticks (2½ pounds), skinned
1½ cups dry whole wheat breadcrumbs
¼ cup grated Parmesan cheese
2 tablespoons minced fresh parsley
¼ teaspoon garlic powder
⅛ teaspoon pepper
⅓ cup skim milk
Vegetable cooking spray

Rinse chicken with cold water, and pat dry. Combine breadcrumbs and next 4 ingredients, stirring well. Dip drumsticks in skim milk. Dredge in breadcrumb mixture, coating well. Place drumsticks in a 10- x 6- x 2-inch baking dish coated with cooking spray. Bake at 350° for 1 hour or until tender. Yield: 4 servings (286 calories per serving).

PROTEIN 37.3 / FAT 8.7 / CARBOHYDRATE 13.4 / CHOLESTEROL 110 / IRON 2.1 / SODIUM 343 / CALCIUM 135

SCAMPI-STYLE CHICKEN THIGHS

4 (6-ounce) chicken thighs, skinned
⅓ cup freshly squeezed lemon juice
2 tablespoons minced fresh parsley
2 tablespoons Chablis or other dry white wine
1 tablespoon margarine, melted
1 tablespoon olive oil
1 clove garlic, minced
⅛ teaspoon onion powder
⅛ teaspoon paprika
Vegetable cooking spray
Lemon wedges (optional)
Fresh parsley sprigs (optional)

Trim excess fat from chicken. Rinse chicken with cold water, and pat dry. Place chicken in a shallow container. Pour lemon juice over chicken, and let stand 20 minutes.

Combine parsley and next 6 ingredients in a small bowl; stir well. Coat rack of a broiler pan with cooking spray. Remove chicken from lemon juice, discarding lemon juice. Arrange chicken on rack, and brush with parsley mixture. Broil 6 inches from heating element 4 minutes on each side or until tender.

Transfer chicken to a serving platter. Garnish with lemon wedges and parsley, if desired. Yield: 4 servings (218 calories per serving).

PROTEIN 19.4 / FAT 14.3 / CARBOHYDRATE 2.6 / CHOLESTEROL 70 / IRON 1.1 / SODIUM 100 / CALCIUM 16

APRICOT CHICKEN THIGHS

½ cup apricot nectar
¼ cup dry sherry
2 tablespoons reduced-sodium soy sauce
1 tablespoon lemon juice
1 tablespoon prepared mustard
½ teaspoon ground ginger
6 chicken thighs (2 pounds), skinned
12 dried apricot halves

Combine first 6 ingredients, mixing well. Set aside.

Trim excess fat from chicken. Rinse chicken with cold water, and pat dry. Place chicken in a 12- x 8- x 2-inch baking dish. Pour reserved apricot nectar mixture over chicken. Cover and bake at 350° for 45 minutes. Uncover, and place apricot halves in apricot nectar mixture. Continue baking, uncovered, 15 minutes or until chicken is tender.

Remove chicken to a warmed serving platter, discarding apricot nectar mixture. Garnish each thigh with 2 apricot halves. Serve immediately. Yield: 6 servings (192 calories per serving).

PROTEIN 18.8 / FAT 7.7 / CARBOHYDRATE 8.5 / CHOLESTEROL 65 / IRON 1.3 / SODIUM 290 / CALCIUM 16

CHICKEN THIGHS MARENGO

6 chicken thighs (2 pounds), skinned
½ teaspoon salt
¼ teaspoon pepper
Vegetable cooking spray
2 teaspoons olive oil
1 cup sliced fresh mushrooms
4 green onions, sliced
1 clove garlic, minced
½ cup Chablis or other dry white wine
¼ teaspoon dried whole thyme or 1 teaspoon chopped
  fresh thyme
2 medium tomatoes, cut into wedges
1 tablespoon minced fresh parsley

Trim excess fat from chicken. Rinse chicken with cold water, and pat dry. Place chicken in a shallow container. Sprinkle with salt and pepper.

Coat a large skillet with cooking spray; add olive oil. Place over medium-high heat until hot. Add chicken to skillet; cook 2 to 3 minutes on each side or until lightly browned. Remove chicken from skillet, and drain on paper towels.

Wipe skillet dry with a paper towel. Recoat skillet with cooking spray; place over medium-high heat until hot. Add mushrooms and cook 2 minutes, stirring frequently. Remove mushrooms from skillet, and set aside.

Recoat skillet with cooking spray. Place over medium-high heat until hot. Add green onions and garlic; sauté 1 minute. Stir in wine and thyme. Add reserved chicken. Bring mixture to a boil. Cover; reduce heat, and simmer 25 minutes. Add reserved mushrooms and tomato wedges; simmer 2 minutes or until thoroughly heated. Sprinkle with parsley, and serve immediately. Yield: 6 servings (175 calories per serving).

PROTEIN 18.6 / FAT 9.2 / CARBOHYDRATE 3.9 / CHOLESTEROL 65 / IRON 1.4 / SODIUM 262 / CALCIUM 20

SPICY CHICKEN STRIP CASSEROLE

1 pound boneless chicken breast halves, skinned
Vegetable cooking spray
2 teaspoons vegetable oil
1 cup frozen whole kernel corn, thawed and drained
½ cup thinly sliced onion
½ cup no-salt-added tomato sauce
2 tablespoons water
1½ teaspoons minced fresh cilantro
1 teaspoon chili powder
½ medium-size green pepper, seeded and chopped
2 tablespoons plus 1½ teaspoons reduced-calorie
  no-salt-added chili sauce
½ cup (2 ounces) shredded Monterey Jack cheese with
  jalapeño peppers

Trim excess fat from chicken. Rinse chicken with cold water, and pat dry. Cut chicken into 3- x ½-inch strips. Coat a large skillet with cooking spray; add vegetable oil. Place over medium-high heat until hot. Add chicken strips, and cook 4 minutes or until chicken is browned, stirring frequently. Remove chicken from skillet, and drain on paper towels.

Combine chicken strips, corn, onion, tomato sauce, water, cilantro, chili powder, green pepper, and chili sauce in a large bowl; stir well. Spoon mixture into a 1½-quart casserole coated with cooking spray. Cover and bake at 350° for 35 minutes. Uncover; sprinkle with cheese, and bake an additional 5 minutes or until cheese melts. Yield: 4 servings (268 calories per serving).

PROTEIN 31.0 / FAT 9.7 / CARBOHYDRATE 14.2 / CHOLESTEROL 81 / IRON 1.4 / SODIUM 159 / CALCIUM 126

MANDARIN CHICKEN BREASTS

4 (4-ounce) boneless chicken breast halves, skinned
Vegetable cooking spray
2 teaspoons vegetable oil
1 (11-ounce) can unsweetened mandarin oranges,
  undrained
2 tablespoons firmly packed brown sugar
1 teaspoon prepared mustard
3 tablespoons reduced-calorie catsup
1 tablespoon vinegar
1 teaspoon cornstarch
½ teaspoon ground cinnamon
⅛ teaspoon ground cloves

Trim excess fat from chicken. Rinse chicken with cold water, and pat dry. Coat a large skillet with cooking spray; add vegetable oil. Place skillet over medium-high heat until hot. Add chicken to skillet; cook 2 to 3 minutes on each side or until lightly browned.

Drain oranges, reserving juice. Set oranges aside. Combine juice and remaining ingredients; stir well, and pour over chicken in skillet. Cover and simmer 30 minutes. Add reserved mandarin oranges, and simmer an additional 5 minutes or until chicken is tender. Transfer to a serving platter, and serve immediately. Yield: 4 servings (216 calories per serving).

PROTEIN 25.8 / FAT 5.3 / CARBOHYDRATE 14.1 / CHOLESTEROL 70 / IRON 1.5 / SODIUM 89 / CALCIUM 23

SOUTHWESTERN CHICKEN KIEV

3 tablespoons margarine, softened
3 tablespoons (¾ ounce) shredded Monterey Jack cheese
  with jalapeño peppers
2 tablespoons minced fresh cilantro
1 teaspoon minced onion
¼ teaspoon garlic powder
Dash of pepper
6 (4-ounce) boneless chicken breast halves, skinned
⅓ cup fine, dry breadcrumbs
½ teaspoon chili powder
¼ cup skim milk
Vegetable cooking spray
3 cups finely shredded iceberg lettuce
1 large tomato, cut into 8 wedges
Fresh cilantro sprigs

Combine first 6 ingredients in a small bowl; stir well. Shape mixture into a 3- x 2-inch stick. Cover and freeze 30 minutes or until firm.

Trim excess fat from chicken. Rinse chicken with cold water, and pat dry. Place chicken between 2 sheets of wax paper; flatten to ¼-inch thickness, using a meat mallet or rolling pin.

Remove margarine stick from freezer, and cut crosswise into 6 portions; place one portion in center of each chicken breast half. Fold long sides of chicken over margarine; fold ends over, and secure with wooden picks.

Combine breadcrumbs and chili powder. Dip each chicken breast half in skim milk, and coat with breadcrumb mixture. Place chicken, seam side up, in a 12- x 8- x 2-inch baking dish coated with cooking spray. Bake at 400° for 15 minutes; turn chicken rolls, and bake an additional 15 minutes or until chicken is tender.

To serve, place shredded lettuce on a serving platter. Top with chicken, and garnish with tomato wedges and cilantro sprigs. Yield: 6 servings (240 calories per serving).

PROTEIN 28.4 / FAT 10.2 / CARBOHYDRATE 7.6 / CHOLESTEROL 74 / IRON 1.5 / SODIUM 202 / CALCIUM 71

GRECIAN-GRILLED CHICKEN

4 (4-ounce) boneless chicken breast halves, skinned
¼ cup fresh lemon juice
3 tablespoons olive oil
2 cloves garlic, crushed
½ teaspoon dried whole oregano
¼ teaspoon salt
¼ teaspoon pepper
Vegetable cooking spray

Trim excess fat from chicken. Rinse chicken with cold water, and pat dry. Place chicken in a 10- x 6- x 2-inch baking dish, and set aside.

Combine lemon juice and next 5 ingredients in a small bowl; stir well. Pour lemon juice marinade over reserved chicken. Cover and refrigerate 2 hours.

Remove chicken from marinade, reserving marinade in baking dish. Coat grill with cooking spray. Grill chicken 4 to 5 inches over medium-hot coals 15 minutes or until chicken is tender, turning and basting with reserved marinade frequently during grilling. Yield: 4 servings (233 calories per serving).

PROTEIN 25.9 / FAT 13.1 / CARBOHYDRATE 2.0 / CHOLESTEROL 70 / IRON 1.0 / SODIUM 208 / CALCIUM 21

FRUIT-STUFFED CHICKEN ROLLS

½ cup cored, peeled, sliced Granny Smith apple
½ cup mixed dried fruit bits
⅓ cup Chablis or other dry white wine
⅓ cup peach brandy
¼ cup unsweetened apple juice
4 (4-ounce) boneless chicken breast halves, skinned
Vegetable cooking spray
2 teaspoons margarine
3 tablespoons skim milk
⅛ teaspoon salt
¼ teaspoon pepper

Combine apple and dried fruit in a small bowl; set aside. Combine wine, brandy, and apple juice in a saucepan; bring to a boil. Boil 2 minutes, stirring occasionally. Pour over reserved fruit mixture; let stand at room temperature 1 to 2 hours.

Trim excess fat from chicken. Rinse chicken with cold water, and pat dry. Place chicken between 2 sheets of wax paper; flatten to ¼-inch thickness, using a meat mallet or rolling pin. Set aside.

Drain fruit mixture, reserving marinade. Spoon ¼ cup fruit mixture onto center of each chicken breast half; roll up lengthwise, tucking edges under. Secure with wooden picks.

Coat a large skillet with cooking spray; add margarine, and place over medium-high heat until margarine melts. Add chicken rolls, and cook until browned on all sides. Add ¼ cup reserved marinade. Cover; reduce heat, and simmer 45 minutes or until chicken is tender. Transfer chicken to a serving platter, and keep warm. Add remaining marinade to skillet; bring to a boil and boil 2 minutes. Reduce heat and stir in skim milk; simmer 5 minutes. Stir in salt and pepper. Spoon sauce over chicken. Yield: 4 servings (268 calories per serving).

PROTEIN 26.8 / FAT 4.9 / CARBOHYDRATE 15.2 / CHOLESTEROL 71 / IRON 1.3 / SODIUM 177 / CALCIUM 32

APPLE-STUFFED CHICKEN ROLLS

Vegetable cooking spray
¼ cup finely chopped green onions
1 cup unsweetened apple juice, divided
½ cup peeled, finely chopped apple
½ cup soft rye breadcrumbs
2 tablespoons minced fresh parsley
⅛ teaspoon salt
⅛ teaspoon caraway seeds
4 (4-ounce) skinned, boned chicken breast halves
2 teaspoons reduced-calorie margarine
2 tablespoons brandy
1 tablespoon cornstarch
Apple slices (optional)

Coat a large nonstick skillet with cooking spray; place over medium-high heat until hot. Add green onions, and sauté until tender. Remove from heat. Stir in 2 tablespoons apple juice and next 5 ingredients. Remove from skillet, and set aside. Wipe pan drippings from skillet with a paper towel.

Place chicken between 2 sheets of wax paper; flatten to ¼-inch thickness, using a meat mallet or rolling pin. Divide breadcrumb mixture evenly among chicken breast halves, spooning mixture into center of each half. Roll breast up lengthwise, tucking ends under. Secure with wooden picks.

Coat skillet with cooking spray; add margarine, and place over medium-high heat until hot. Add chicken rolls, and cook until browned on all sides. Add 2 tablespoons apple juice and brandy. Cover, reduce heat, and simmer 45 minutes, or until chicken is tender. Transfer chicken to a serving platter; remove wooden picks, and keep warm.

Add cornstarch to pan juices in skillet; stir until smooth. Stir in remaining ¾ cup apple juice. Bring to a boil; cook 1 minute or until thickened and bubbly. Spoon sauce over chicken rolls. Garnish with apple slices, if desired. Yield: 4 servings (202 calories per serving).

PROTEIN 27.1 / FAT 3.0 / CARBOHYDRATE 15.6 / CHOLESTEROL 66 / IRON 1.4 / SODIUM 208 / CALCIUM 30

CRANBERRY CHICKEN CUTLETS

4 (4-ounce) boneless chicken breast halves, skinned
¼ cup all-purpose flour
⅛ teaspoon salt
¼ teaspoon pepper
Vegetable cooking spray
1 tablespoon margarine
¾ cup cranberry juice cocktail
⅓ cup fresh or frozen cranberries, thawed
⅛ teaspoon ground cinnamon
Dash of ground cloves
2 tablespoons cold water
2 teaspoons cornstarch
1 teaspoon sugar

Trim excess fat from chicken. Rinse chicken with cold water, and pat dry. Place chicken between 2 sheets of wax paper; flatten to ¼-inch thickness, using a meat mallet or rolling pin. Combine flour, salt, and pepper; stir well. Dredge chicken in flour mixture.

Coat a large skillet with cooking spray; add margarine, and place over medium-high heat until margarine melts. Add chicken, and cook 3 minutes on each side or until browned. Remove chicken from skillet, and drain well on paper towels. Transfer chicken to a serving platter, and keep warm.

Combine cranberry juice cocktail, cranberries, cinnamon, and cloves in a small saucepan. Bring to a boil; reduce heat, and simmer, uncovered, 2 minutes or until cranberries burst. Combine the water, cornstarch, and sugar, stirring until blended. Pour cornstarch mixture into cranberry mixture; cook over medium-high heat, stirring constantly, until mixture thickens. Remove from heat, and spoon sauce over chicken. Serve immediately. Yield: 4 servings (235 calories per serving).

PROTEIN 26.7 / FAT 5.9 / CARBOHYDRATE 17.1 / CHOLESTEROL 70 / IRON 1.2 / SODIUM 170 / CALCIUM 19

CHINESE CHICKEN BARBECUE

---

4 (6-ounce) chicken breast halves, skinned
½ cup reduced-calorie catsup
2 tablespoons firmly packed brown sugar
2 tablespoons reduced-sodium soy sauce
½ teaspoon ground ginger
1 clove garlic, minced
Vegetable cooking spray
Minced fresh parsley (optional)

Trim excess fat from chicken. Rinse chicken with cold water, and pat dry. Place chicken in a 10- x 6- x 2-inch baking dish. Combine catsup, brown sugar, soy sauce, ginger, and garlic, stirring well. Pour over chicken, turning chicken to coat well. Cover and marinate in refrigerator at least 2 hours.

Remove chicken from marinade, reserving marinade. Place chicken on a rack in a roasting pan coated with cooking spray. Brush chicken with 2 tablespoons marinade.

Bake at 350° for 40 minutes, basting with marinade every 20 minutes. Transfer to a serving platter, and sprinkle chicken with minced parsley, if desired. Yield: 4 servings (193 calories per serving).

PROTEIN 27.8 / FAT 3.1 / CARBOHYDRATE 10.3 / CHOLESTEROL 74 / IRON 1.2 / SODIUM 365 / CALCIUM 21

ORANGE SKILLET CHICKEN

1 (3½-pound) broiler fryer, cut up and skinned
Vegetable cooking spray
2 teaspoons vegetable oil
¼ cup brandy
¾ cup unsweetened orange juice
½ cup plus tablespoon water, divided
¼ teaspoon salt
⅛ teaspoon white pepper
¼ cup Grand Marnier or other orange-flavored liqueur
¼ cup reduced-calorie orange marmalade
1 teaspoon lemon juice
2 teaspoons cornstarch

Trim excess fat from chicken. Rinse chicken with cold water; pat dry. Coat a large skillet with cooking spray; add vegetable oil, and place over medium-high heat until hot. Add chicken and cook until lightly browned on all sides. Remove chicken; drain on paper towels.

Wipe skillet with a paper towel. Return chicken to skillet. Add brandy, and heat just until warm (do not boil). Ignite brandy with a long-handled match. When flames die, add orange juice, ½ cup water, salt, and white pepper, stirring well. Cover; reduce heat, and simmer 20 minutes. Add Grand Marnier, marmalade, and lemon juice. Cover and simmer 10 minutes, basting occasionally. Remove chicken to a serving platter, and keep warm.

Combine cornstarch and remaining 1 tablespoon water, stirring until blended. Pour cornstarch mixture into chicken liquid; cook over medium-high heat, stirring constantly, until thickened. Remove from heat, and spoon orange juice mixture over chicken. Serve immediately. Yield: 8 servings (209 calories per serving).

PROTEIN 20.6 / FAT 6.4 / CARBOHYDRATE 8.3 / CHOLESTEROL 63 / IRON 0.9 / SODIUM 134 / CALCIUM 13

ARROZ CON POLLO

1 (3½-pound) broiler fryer, cut up and skinned
Vegetable cooking spray
1 teaspoon vegetable oil
2 cups water
1 (14½-ounce) can no-salt-added stewed tomatoes,
    undrained and chopped
1 cup chopped onion
2 teaspoons chicken-flavored bouillon granules
1 clove garlic, minced
1 medium-size jalapeño pepper, minced
¼ teaspoon powdered saffron
⅛ teaspoon pepper
1 cup regular rice, uncooked
¼ cup sliced pimiento-stuffed olives, drained
2 tablespoons lime juice

Trim excess fat from chicken. Rinse chicken with cold water; pat
dry. Coat a 12-inch skillet with cooking spray; add vegetable oil,
and place over medium-high heat until hot. Add chicken, and cook
4 minutes on each side or until browned. Remove chicken; drain
on paper towels.

Wipe skillet with a paper towel; recoat with cooking spray. Add
chicken to skillet. Combine the water and next 7 ingredients; pour
over chicken. Cover and cook over medium heat 15 minutes. Add
rice; cover and cook over medium heat 20 minutes or until tender.
Remove from heat, and stir in olives; sprinkle with lime juice.
Yield: 6 servings (347 calories per serving).

PROTEIN 30.7 / FAT 8.8 / CARBOHYDRATE 34.5 / CHOLESTEROL 84 / IRON 2.8 / SODIUM 358 /
CALCIUM 54

ROAST CHICKEN WITH YOGURT GRAVY

1 (3½-pound) broiler fryer, skinned
½ small lemon, cut into wedges
¼ cup water
⅓ cup reduced-calorie Italian salad dressing
⅛ teaspoon pepper
Yogurt Gravy (recipe follows)

Remove giblets and neck from chicken, and reserve for other uses. Trim excess fat from chicken. Rinse chicken with cold water, and pat dry. Place lemon wedges in cavity of chicken. Close cavity with skewers, and truss. Lift wingtips up and over back, tucking under bird securely. Place chicken, breast side up, on a rack in a roasting pan. Pour ¼ cup water in bottom of pan. Set aside.

Combine salad dressing and pepper, stirring well. Brush half of dressing mixture over entire surface of chicken. Bake chicken, uncovered, at 375° for 1 hour and 15 minutes or until drumsticks move up and down easily and juices run clear. Baste frequently with remaining dressing mixture during cooking. Remove and discard lemon wedges.

Transfer chicken to a serving platter, and top with Yogurt Gravy. Yield: 6 servings (218 calories per serving).

Yogurt Gravy:

1 tablespoon plus 2 teaspoons reduced-calorie Italian
    salad dressing
1 tablespoon all-purpose flour
½ teaspoon chicken-flavored bouillon granules
¼ cup water
1 (8-ounce) carton plain low-fat yogurt

Combine salad dressing, flour, and bouillon granules in a small bowl to form a smooth paste. Place ¼ cup water in a small saucepan. Stir in dressing paste. Cook over medium heat, stirring constantly, until thickened and bubbly. Stir yogurt into mixture. Cook, stirring constantly, until gravy is thoroughly heated. (Do not boil.) Yield: 1 cup.

PROTEIN 29.5 / FAT 7.6 / CARBOHYDRATE 6.5 / CHOLESTEROL 86 / IRON 1.3 / SODIUM 298 / CALCIUM 91

CHICKEN LIVERS IN WINE

1½ pounds chicken livers
½ cup dry white wine
3 tablespoons lemon juice
¼ teaspoon salt
½ teaspoon pepper
Vegetable cooking spray
¼ pound fresh mushrooms, sliced

Combine chicken livers, wine, lemon juice, salt, and pepper in a bowl; cover and marinate in refrigerator 30 minutes.

Coat a large skillet with cooking spray; place over medium heat until hot. Add chicken livers and mushrooms, and sauté 5 minutes or until livers are done. Yield: 4 servings (190 calories per serving).

PROTEIN 25.6 / FAT 5.7 / CARBOHYDRATE 3.6 / FIBER 0.2 / CHOLESTEROL 644 / SODIUM 201 / POTASSIUM 283

GRILLED CHABLIS CHICKEN

---

6 (4-ounce) boneless chicken breast halves, skinned
⅓ cup Chablis or other dry white wine
⅓ cup white wine vinegar
4 green onions with tops, chopped
½ teaspoon dried whole basil
¼ teaspoon pepper
Vegetable cooking spray

Trim excess fat from chicken. Rinse chicken with cold water, and pat dry. Place in a 12- x 8- x 2-inch baking dish. Combine wine, vinegar, green onions, basil, and pepper; stir well. Pour wine mixture over chicken. Cover and marinate in refrigerator 4 hours.

Remove chicken from marinade; discard green onions and reserve marinade. Arrange chicken on a grill coated with cooking spray. Grill 6 inches over hot coals 10 minutes or until chicken is tender, turning and basting with reserved marinade every 3 minutes. Yield: 6 servings (142 calories per serving).

PROTEIN 25.8 / FAT 3.0 / CARBOHYDRATE 0.8 / CHOLESTEROL 70 / IRON 1.0 / SODIUM 64 / CALCIUM 19

CHICKEN WITH APPLEJACK

1 pound medium Granny Smith apples, sliced
Vegetable cooking spray
2 cups sliced onion
4 (4-ounce) boneless chicken breast halves, skinned
2 teaspoons unsalted margarine
¼ cup applejack or apple brandy
1¼ cups water
1 teaspoon chicken-flavored bouillon granules

Cook apples in a skillet coated with cooking spray over medium heat 3 minutes; transfer to a bowl. Cook onion in a skillet coated with cooking spray over medium heat 7 minutes or until tender. Transfer to the bowl with apples.

Cook chicken in margarine in a skillet coated with cooking spray over medium-high heat 2 minutes on each side. Transfer chicken to a plate, and set aside. Add apples, onion, applejack, water, and bouillon granules to skillet, and cook over medium-high heat until mixture is reduced by half. Add chicken, and cook 1 minute or until done. Transfer to a serving platter. Yield: 4 servings (245 calories per serving).

PROTEIN 26.7 / FAT 5.8 / CARBOHYDRATE 22.1 / FIBER 3.2 / CHOLESTEROL 70 / SODIUM 159 / POTASSIUM 447

WILD RICE AND CHICKEN CASSEROLE

1 (6-ounce) package long-grain and wild rice mix
2 tablespoons unsalted margarine
2 tablespoons all-purpose flour
1 cup skim milk
¼ cup Chablis or other dry white wine
Vegetable cooking spray
½ cup sliced fresh mushrooms
½ cup sliced green onion
4 cups chopped, cooked chicken or turkey breast (skinned
  before cooking and cooked without salt)
1 (2-ounce) jar diced pimiento, drained
2 tablespoons chopped fresh parsley

Cook rice mix according to package directions, omitting fat; set
aside.

Melt margarine in a small heavy saucepan over low heat; add
flour, stirring until smooth. Cook 1 minute, stirring constantly.
Gradually add skim milk; cook over medium heat, stirring constantly, until thickened and bubbly. Remove from heat, and stir in
wine. Set aside.

Coat a small skillet with cooking spray; place over medium heat
until hot. Add mushrooms and green onion, and sauté 2 to 3
minutes or until tender.

Combine sautéed vegetables, rice, sauce, chicken, pimiento,
and parsley, stirring well. Spoon mixture into a 2-quart casserole
coated with cooking spray. Bake at 350° for 15 minutes or until
thoroughly heated. Yield: 8 servings (240 calories per serving).

PROTEIN 25.6 / FAT 5.6 / CARBOHYDRATE 20.6 / FIBER 0.5 / CHOLESTEROL 60 / SODIUM 436 /
POTASSIUM 366

ITALIAN-STYLE CHICKEN AND PEPPERS

½ cup fine, dry breadcrumbs
½ teaspoon dried Italian seasoning
¼ teaspoon dried whole basil
¼ teaspoon salt
⅛ teaspoon pepper
4 (6-ounce) chicken thighs, skinned
1 egg, lightly beaten
Vegetable cooking spray
1 teaspoon olive or vegetable oil
1 medium-size green pepper, seeded and cut into
    1-inch-wide strips
1 medium-size red pepper, seeded and cut into
    1-inch-wide strips
1 clove garlic, minced
¼ cup Burgundy or other dry red wine
1 tablespoon red wine vinegar
1 tablespoon grated Parmesan cheese

Combine first 5 ingredients in a small bowl; stir well, and set aside.
  Trim excess fat from chicken. Dip chicken in egg; dredge in breadcrumb mixture.
  Coat a large skillet with cooking spray; add olive oil. Place skillet over medium-high heat until hot. Add chicken to skillet; cook 2 to 3 minutes on each side or until lightly browned. Remove from skillet, and arrange in a 9-inch square baking dish coated with cooking spray. Cover and bake at 350° for 1 hour. Remove to a warm platter; set aside, and keep warm.
  Wipe pan drippings from skillet with a paper towel; coat skillet with cooking spray. Add pepper strips and garlic to skillet; sauté until tender. Stir in wine and vinegar; simmer 2 minutes. Spoon mixture over chicken, and sprinkle with Parmesan cheese. Yield: 4 servings (263 calories per serving).

PROTEIN 24.3 / FAT 12.2 / CARBOHYDRATE 12.9 / FIBER 0.6 / CHOLESTEROL 144 / SODIUM 350 / POTASSIUM 337

PINEAPPLE-GRILLED CHICKEN

6 chicken thighs (2 pounds), skinned
1 (8-ounce) can unsweetened pineapple tidbits, undrained
¼ cup reduced-sodium soy sauce
⅓ cup dry sherry
1 tablespoon firmly packed brown sugar
1 teaspoon dry mustard
Vegetable cooking spray
¼ cup water
2 teaspoons cornstarch

Trim excess fat from chicken; place chicken in a 12- x 8- x 2-inch baking dish, and set aside.

Drain pineapple, reserving juice; set pineapple aside. Combine pineapple juice, soy sauce, sherry, brown sugar, and dry mustard in a small bowl; stir well. Reserve ¼ cup marinade; pour remaining marinade over chicken. Cover and refrigerate 2 hours.

Remove chicken from marinade, reserving marinade in baking dish. Coat grill with cooking spray. Grill chicken 6 inches over medium coals 40 minutes or until chicken is tender, turning and basting with marinade in baking dish every 10 minutes. Transfer to a serving platter, and keep warm.

Place reserved ¼ cup marinade in a small saucepan. Combine water and cornstarch; stir into marinade. Bring to a boil over medium heat. Boil 1 minute or until mixture is thickened, stirring constantly; stir in reserved pineapple, and cook just until thoroughly heated. Spoon sauce over chicken to serve. Yield: 6 servings (196 calories per serving).

PROTEIN 18.9 / FAT 7.6 / CARBOHYDRATE 8.2 / FIBER 0.1 / CHOLESTEROL 65 / SODIUM 451 / POTASSIUM 219

CHICKEN BREASTS STUFFED WITH HERB CHEESE

½ (8-ounce) package Neufchâtel cheese, softened
1 tablespoon chopped fresh parsley
½ teaspoon lemon-pepper seasoning
¼ teaspoon dried whole basil
¼ teaspoon dried whole oregano
Dash of garlic powder
8 (4-ounce) boneless chicken breast halves, skinned
1 egg, beaten
2 tablespoons water
½ cup fine, dry breadcrumbs

Combine Neufchâtel, parsley, lemon-pepper seasoning, basil, oregano, and garlic powder in a small bowl; stir well. Set mixture aside.

Trim excess fat from chicken. Place each piece of chicken between 2 sheets of waxed paper; flatten to ¼-inch thickness, using a meat mallet or rolling pin.

Place equal portions of cheese mixture in center of each piece of chicken; roll up jelly roll fashion. Tuck in sides; secure with wooden picks.

Combine egg and water in a small bowl; stir well. Dip each roll in egg mixture; dredge in breadcrumbs. Place rolls in a 12- x 8- x 2-inch baking dish. Bake at 400° for 30 minutes. Remove wooden picks to serve. Yield: 8 servings (208 calories per serving).

PROTEIN 28.7 / FAT 7.3 / CARBOHYDRATE 5.2 / FIBER 0.0 / CHOLESTEROL 116 / SODIUM 173 / POTASSIUM 250

CHICKEN FAJITAS

2 pounds boneless chicken breast halves, skinned
¼ cup white wine vinegar
¼ cup lime juice
2 tablespoons Worcestershire sauce
2 tablespoons chopped onion
2 cloves garlic, minced
1 teaspoon dried whole oregano
¼ teaspoon ground cumin
Vegetable cooking spray
8 (8-inch) flour tortillas
½ cup picante sauce, divided
½ cup plain low-fat yogurt, divided
¼ cup chopped green chiles, divided

Trim excess fat from chicken. Place chicken between 2 sheets of waxed paper; flatten to ¼-inch thickness, using a meat mallet or rolling pin. Place chicken in a 13- x 9- x 2-inch baking dish. Combine vinegar, lime juice, Worcestershire sauce, onion, garlic, oregano, and cumin; pour over chicken. Cover and refrigerate 4 hours.

Remove chicken from marinade, discarding marinade; arrange chicken on a grill coated with cooking spray. Grill 6 inches over medium-hot coals 8 minutes, turning once. Slice chicken across the grain into ½-inch-wide strips.

Wrap tortillas in aluminum foil; bake at 325° for 15 minutes. Arrange strips of chicken just off center of each tortilla; roll up tortillas. Top each with 1 tablespoon picante sauce, 1 tablespoon yogurt, and 1½ teaspoons green chiles. Yield: 8 servings (308 calories per serving).

PROTEIN 30.1 / FAT 5.6 / CARBOHYDRATE 33.7 / FIBER 0.4 / CHOLESTEROL 71 / SODIUM 224 / POTASSIUM 346

YOGURT-MARINATED CHICKEN

6 chicken breast halves (about 2½ pounds), skinned
1 (8-ounce) carton plain low-fat yogurt
¼ cup lemon juice
1 tablespoon Worcestershire sauce
1 teaspoon paprika
½ teaspoon pepper
¼ teaspoon garlic powder
¼ teaspoon celery salt
¾ cup soft whole wheat breadcrumbs
Vegetable cooking spray

Trim excess fat from chicken; place chicken in a single layer in a 13- x 9- x 2-inch baking dish. Combine next 7 ingredients; pour over chicken, turning to coat well. Cover and refrigerate 8 hours or overnight, turning occasionally.

Remove chicken from marinade, discarding marinade. Dredge chicken in breadcrumbs.

Arrange chicken in a 13- x 9- x 2-inch baking dish coated with cooking spray. Bake at 375° for 45 minutes or until chicken is tender. Yield: 6 servings (190 calories per serving).

PROTEIN 29.9 / FAT 4.0 / CARBOHYDRATE 7.4 / FIBER 0.4 / CHOLESTEROL 77 / SODIUM 236 / POTASSIUM 375

ROASTED CHICKEN AND VEGETABLES

1 (3½-pound) broiler-fryer, skinned
1 medium cooking apple, cut into wedges
½ cup water
2 tablespoons lemon juice
2 tablespoons chopped fresh parsley
1 tablespoon prepared mustard
1 teaspoon chicken-flavored bouillon granules
1 teaspoon ground ginger
½ teaspoon ground cinnamon
½ teaspoon pepper
2 medium-size sweet potatoes, peeled and cut into thirds
3 medium onions, quartered

Remove giblets and neck from chicken, and reserve for other uses. Trim excess fat from chicken. Place apple wedges in cavity of chicken. Close cavity with skewers, and truss. Lift wingtips up and over back, tucking under bird securely. Place chicken, breast side up, on a rack in a roasting pan; set aside.

Combine the water, lemon juice, parsley, mustard, bouillon granules, ginger, cinnamon, and pepper; brush over entire surface of chicken. Arrange sweet potatoes and onions around chicken. Cover and bake at 350° for 1½ hours or until drumsticks move up and down easily and juices run clear. Discard apple wedges.

Remove chicken and vegetables to a serving platter; serve immediately. Yield: 6 servings (272 calories per serving).

PROTEIN 29.3 / FAT 7.6 / CARBOHYDRATE 21.0 / FIBER 2.0 / CHOLESTEROL 84 / SODIUM 187 / POTASSIUM 486

CRISPY OVEN-FRIED CHICKEN

1 egg, lightly beaten
1 tablespoon water
1 cup crispy rice cereal, crushed
¼ cup buttermilk baking mix
1 tablespoon instant minced onion
¼ teaspoon garlic powder
¼ teaspoon seasoned salt
¼ teaspoon pepper
1 (3½-pound) broiler-fryer, cut up and skinned
Vegetable cooking spray
Green onion fans (optional)
Carrot flowers (optional)

Combine egg and 1 tablespoon water in a shallow bowl; mix well, and set aside.

Combine crushed cereal, baking mix, minced onion, garlic powder, seasoned salt, and pepper in a shallow bowl; stir until well blended, and set aside.

Trim excess fat from chicken; dip chicken in egg mixture, and dredge in cereal mixture, coating well. Arrange chicken in a 15- x 10- x 1-inch jelly roll pan coated with cooking spray. Bake, uncovered, at 350° for 1 hour or until tender. Transfer to a serving platter, and garnish with green onion fans and carrot flowers, if desired. Yield: 6 servings (242 calories per serving).

PROTEIN 29.2 / FAT 8.9 / CARBOHYDRATE 9.4 / FIBER 0.3 / CHOLESTEROL 129 / SODIUM 284 / POTASSIUM 266

CREOLE CHICKEN EN PAPILLOTE

Vegetable cooking spray
½ cup chopped onion
½ cup chopped green onion
½ cup chopped celery
½ cup chopped green pepper
2 cloves garlic, minced
1 (16-ounce) can tomatoes, undrained and chopped
1 (6-ounce) can tomato paste
¼ cup water
½ teaspoon dried whole basil
½ teaspoon dried whole thyme
½ teaspoon red pepper
½ teaspoon hot sauce
1 bay leaf
6 (4-ounce) boneless chicken breast halves, skinned
Parchment paper

Coat a large skillet with cooking spray; place over medium-high heat until hot. Add onion, green onion, celery, green pepper, and garlic; sauté until tender. Add tomatoes, tomato paste, water, basil, thyme, red pepper, hot sauce, and bay leaf. Bring to a boil; reduce heat, and simmer, uncovered, 20 minutes. Discard bay leaf; set sauce aside.

Trim excess fat from chicken breast halves. Place chicken between 2 sheets of waxed paper; flatten to ¼-inch thickness, using a meat mallet or rolling pin.

Cut 6 15- x 14-inch pieces of parchment paper; fold each piece of paper in half lengthwise, creasing the fold firmly. Cut each paper to form a large heart shape; place paper hearts on 2 baking sheets, and open out flat.

Place a chicken breast half on each parchment paper heart near crease. Spoon sauce in equal portions over each breast half. Fold paper edges over to seal securely; starting with rounded edge of heart, pleat and crimp edges of each heart to make an airtight seal.

Bake at 450° for 15 minutes or until pouches are puffed and browned. Place on individual serving plates; cut an opening in each pouch just before serving. Yield: 6 servings (191 calories per serving).

PROTEIN 28.0 / FAT 3.6 / CARBOHYDRATE 12.0 / FIBER 6.3 / CHOLESTEROL 70 / SODIUM 216 / POTASSIUM 748

ORANGE-GLAZED CHICKEN KABOBS

2 tablespoons reduced-sodium soy sauce
1 tablespoon honey
2 teaspoons cornstarch
1 teaspoon grated orange rind
¾ cup unsweetened orange juice
¼ teaspoon ground ginger
1 pound boneless chicken breast halves, skinned
8 whole water chestnuts
3 green onions, cut into 2-inch pieces
12 medium-size fresh mushrooms
Vegetable cooking spray

Combine first 6 ingredients in a nonaluminum saucepan. Bring to a boil; reduce heat, and cook over low heat, stirring constantly, 1 minute or until mixture thickens. Set aside to cool.

Trim excess fat from chicken; cut chicken into 1-inch pieces, and place in a 12- x 8- x 2-inch baking dish. Pour reserved soy sauce mixture over chicken; cover and marinate in refrigerator overnight.

Remove chicken from marinade, reserving marinade. Alternate chicken pieces, water chestnuts, green onions, and mushrooms on 4 skewers. Coat grill with cooking spray. Grill kabobs 6 inches over medium coals 15 minutes or until done, turning and basting often with marinade. Yield: 4 servings (220 calories per serving).

PROTEIN 28.1 / FAT 3.3 / CARBOHYDRATE 18.8 / FIBER 0.8 / CHOLESTEROL 70 / SODIUM 358 / POTASSIUM 614

ZESTY BARBECUED CHICKEN

1 (3½-pound) broiler-fryer, cut up and skinned
1 (8-ounce) can tomato sauce
½ teaspoon grated lemon rind
¼ cup lemon juice
1 tablespoon firmly packed brown sugar
2 tablespoons vinegar
1 tablespoon Worcestershire sauce
1 teaspoon prepared mustard
¼ teaspoon red pepper
¼ teaspoon pepper
1 clove garlic, crushed

Trim excess fat from chicken; place chicken in 12- x 8- x 2-inch baking dish, and set aside.

Combine remaining ingredients in a small saucepan. Bring to a boil. Cover; reduce heat, and simmer 20 minutes. Pour barbecue sauce over chicken. Cover and marinate in refrigerator overnight, turning chicken occasionally.

Remove chicken from sauce, reserving sauce. Place chicken, bone side down, on grill over medium coals. Grill 45 minutes to 1 hour, turning and basting with sauce every 15 minutes. Yield: 6 servings (207 calories per serving).

PROTEIN 28.0 / FAT 7.0 / CARBOHYDRATE 7.2 / FIBER 0.3 / CHOLESTEROL 84 / SODIUM 284 / POTASSIUM 459

MEXICAN-STYLE CHICKEN ROLL-UPS

8 (4-ounce) boneless chicken breast halves, skinned
4 canned whole green chiles, halved and seeded
3 ounces Monterey Jack cheese, cut into 8 strips
¾ cup fine, dry breadcrumbs
1 tablespoon chili powder
1½ teaspoons ground cumin
¼ teaspoon salt
¼ teaspoon garlic powder
¼ cup skim milk
Vegetable cooking spray
4 cups shredded lettuce
½ cup commercial picante sauce
¼ cup plain low-fat yogurt

Trim excess fat from chicken. Place each chicken breast half between 2 sheets of waxed paper; flatten to ¼-inch thickness, using a meat mallet or rolling pin.

Place a green chile half and one strip of cheese in center of each chicken breast half; roll up lengthwise, tucking edges under. Secure with wooden picks.

Combine breadcrumbs, chili powder, cumin, salt, and garlic powder. Dip chicken rolls in skim milk; dredge in breadcrumb mixture, coating well. Place chicken in a 12- x 8- x 2-inch baking dish coated with cooking spray. Bake at 400° for 30 minutes or until chicken is done.

Place each chicken roll on ½ cup shredded lettuce; top each with 1 tablespoon picante sauce and 1½ teaspoons yogurt. Serve immediately. Yield: 8 servings (236 calories per serving).

PROTEIN 30.7 / FAT 7.1 / CARBOHYDRATE 10.6 / FIBER 0.7 / CHOLESTEROL 80 / SODIUM 405 / POTASSIUM 392

CHICKEN DIVAN

1 pound fresh broccoli
2 tablespoons unsalted margarine
3 tablespoons all-purpose flour
1 cup water
1 teaspoon chicken-flavored bouillon granules
1 cup skim milk
¼ cup dry white wine
¼ cup plus 2 tablespoons grated Parmesan cheese,
  divided
Vegetable cooking spray
2 cups coarsely chopped, cooked chicken breasts

Trim off large leaves from broccoli. Remove tough ends of stalks, and wash broccoli thoroughly; separate into spears. Arrange broccoli in steaming rack, with stalks to center of rack. Place over boiling water; cover and steam 10 minutes or just until tender.

Melt margarine in a saucepan over low heat; add flour, and stir until smooth. Combine the water and bouillon granules, stirring until dissolved; add skim milk. Gradually add broth mixture to saucepan; cook over medium heat, stirring constantly, until mixture is thickened and bubbly. Gradually add wine and ¼ cup Parmesan cheese, stirring well. Cook over low heat 5 minutes.

Arrange broccoli in a 13- x 9- x 2-inch baking dish coated with cooking spray; top with chicken, and pour sauce over chicken. Sprinkle with remaining 2 tablespoons Parmesan cheese, and bake, uncovered, at 350° for 30 minutes or until top is golden brown. Yield: 6 servings (180 calories per serving).

PROTEIN 20.1 / FAT 6.9 / CARBOHYDRATE 9.9 / FIBER 1.7 / CHOLESTEROL 43 / SODIUM 195 / POTASSIUM 395

PHYLLO CHICKEN POT PIE

2 pounds chicken thighs, skinned, boned, and trimmed of
    fat
1 medium onion, chopped
1 medium-size tart apple, peeled and chopped
2 medium carrots, chopped
1½ cups chopped celery
1 medium-size sweet red or green pepper, chopped
1 cup chopped green onion
¼ teaspoon ground nutmeg
⅛ teaspoon dried whole thyme
⅛ teaspoon pepper
1 cup chicken broth
2 tablespoons cornstarch
2 tablespoons water
1 tablespoon Worcestershire sauce
3 tablespoons minced fresh parsley
Vegetable cooking spray
2 tablespoons unsalted margarine, melted
1 tablespoon lemon juice
8 sheets frozen phyllo or strudel dough, thawed
Additional sheet frozen phyllo or strudel dough, thawed
    (optional)

Cut chicken into 1-inch pieces; combine with next 10 ingredients in
a large Dutch oven. Cook over medium heat 1 hour or until chicken
pieces are tender, stirring frequently.

Combine cornstarch, 2 tablespoons water, and Worcestershire
sauce in a small bowl, stirring until blended; stir into chicken
mixture. Add parsley, and bring to a boil. Reduce heat, and
simmer until sauce thickens, stirring constantly; remove from
heat. Transfer mixture to a 10-inch pie plate coated with cooking
spray.

Combine margarine and lemon juice in a bowl. Place 1 phyllo
sheet on a flat surface; brush lightly with a small amount of
margarine mixture. Repeat procedure with remaining 7 phyllo
sheets, arranging sheets on top of each other to form a stack. Cut
phyllo stack into a 10-inch round, and place over chicken mixture,

pressing dough to edge of pie plate to seal. Cut slits in phyllo. Use additional phyllo sheet to decorate top, if desired. Brush top with remaining margarine mixture. Bake at 350° for 45 minutes or until top of pie is golden brown. Yield: 8 servings (275 calories per serving).

PROTEIN 15.1 / FAT 17.0 / CARBOHYDRATE 15.1 / FIBER 1.6 / CHOLESTEROL 50 / SODIUM 207 / POTASSIUM 394

CURRIED CHICKEN AND RICE

2 stalks celery, chopped
1 medium onion, chopped
1 medium apple, cored and chopped
1 clove garlic, minced
1 teaspoon vegetable oil
Vegetable cooking spray
1 pound boneless chicken breast halves, skinned and cut into 1-inch pieces
1 cup white rice, uncooked
1 cup chopped tomato
¼ cup raisins
1½ teaspoons chicken-flavored bouillon granules
2 teaspoons curry powder
2 cups water
2 tablespoons minced fresh parsley
⅛ teaspoon ground red pepper

Cook first 5 ingredients in an ovenproof ceramic casserole coated with cooking spray over medium heat until softened. Stir in chicken, rice, tomato, raisins, bouillon granules, curry powder, and 2 cups water; bring to a boil. Remove from heat and cover. Transfer to oven, and bake at 350° for 25 to 30 minutes or until broth is absorbed. Stir in parsley and red pepper. Yield: 6 servings (261 calories per serving).

PROTEIN 20.2 / FAT 3.3 / CARBOHYDRATE 37.1 / FIBER 2.3 / CHOLESTEROL 47 / SODIUM 155 / POTASSIUM 400

CITRUS CHICKEN AND VEGETABLES

3 tablespoons unsalted margarine, softened
1 tablespoon minced fresh mint leaves
1 tablespoon minced fresh parsley
1 teaspoon finely grated lemon rind
1 teaspoon finely grated orange rind
1 teaspoon lemon juice
1 clove garlic, minced
4 (4-ounce) boneless chicken breast halves, skinned
2 medium carrots, thinly sliced
½ cup frozen whole kernel corn, thawed
¼ cup chopped green onion

Combine first 7 ingredients in a bowl. Place each chicken breast on a 12-inch square of aluminum foil; spread each piece with one fourth of margarine mixture. Top each with equal amounts of carrots, corn, and green onion. Seal edges of foil tightly; place in a baking pan. Bake at 400° for 20 minutes or until chicken is done. Yield: 4 servings (249 calories per serving).

PROTEIN 26.9 / FAT 11.6 / CARBOHYDRATE 9.2 / FIBER 1.2 / CHOLESTEROL 70 / SODIUM 76 / POTASSIUM 402

BOURBON-MARINATED CHICKEN ROLLS

4 (4-ounce) boneless chicken breast halves, skinned
1¼ teaspoons chicken-flavored bouillon granules
1¼ cups water
⅓ cup minced green onion
¼ cup bourbon (80 proof)
2 tablespoons white wine vinegar
2 tablespoons Dijon mustard
2 teaspoons reduced-sodium soy sauce
⅛ teaspoon dried whole thyme
1 clove garlic, minced

1 bay leaf
2 slices bacon, halved
Vegetable cooking spray
2 teaspoons cornstarch
1 tablespoon water
1 teaspoon Dijon mustard
1 tablespoon minced green onion tops

Place chicken between 2 sheets of waxed paper, and flatten to ¼-inch thickness, using a meat mallet or rolling pin; set aside.

Combine next 11 ingredients in a large shallow dish, mixing well. Add chicken, turning to coat. Cover and marinate in refrigerator at least 2 hours. Transfer chicken to paper towels. Strain marinade into a saucepan; set aside.

Roll up chicken breasts, beginning with a long side; wrap ½ slice bacon around each, and secure with wooden picks. Arrange rolls on a broiler pan coated with cooking spray. Broil 4 to 6 inches from heat 3 to 5 minutes on each side or until bacon is crisp and chicken is done. Transfer rolls to a platter; remove and discard wooden picks. Cover and keep warm.

Bring marinade to a boil. Reduce heat; simmer 5 minutes. Combine cornstarch and 1 tablespoon water in a bowl; add to marinade, and simmer until slightly thickened, stirring constantly. Stir in 1 teaspoon mustard. Spoon sauce over chicken; garnish with green onion. Yield: 4 servings (257 calories per serving).

PROTEIN 28.9 / FAT 12.2 / CARBOHYDRATE 7.7 / FIBER 0.3 / CHOLESTEROL 80 / SODIUM 761 / POTASSIUM 352

STIR-FRIED CHICKEN AND VEGETABLES

2 teaspoons cornstarch
¼ cup plus 1 tablespoon water, divided
Vegetable cooking spray
2 teaspoons sesame oil
1½ pounds boneless chicken breast halves, skinned and
    cut into ¼-inch strips
1 tablespoon minced, peeled gingerroot
3 cups yellow squash, cut into julienne strips
3 cups zucchini, cut into julienne strips
1 cup diagonally sliced green onion
¼ teaspoon chicken-flavored bouillon granules
1 teaspoon reduced-sodium soy sauce
1½ teaspoons dried whole basil or 2 tablespoons minced
    fresh basil
¼ teaspoon salt
⅛ teaspoon crushed red pepper
⅛ teaspoon ground red pepper

Combine cornstarch in 1 tablespoon water in a small bowl, and set aside. Coat a large heavy skillet or wok with cooking spray; add sesame oil, and place over high heat until hot. Add chicken strips and gingerroot; stir-fry 4 to 5 minutes or until chicken is done.

Add yellow squash, zucchini, and green onion; stir-fry 2 minutes. Add remaining ¼ cup water, bouillon granules, soy sauce, and cornstarch mixture; bring to a boil, and cook 1 minute or until thickened, stirring constantly. Stir in remaining ingredients. Serve immediately. Yield: 6 servings (184 calories per serving).

PROTEIN 27.6 / FAT 4.8 / CARBOHYDRATE 7.3 / FIBER 1.6 / CHOLESTEROL 70 / SODIUM 212 / POTASSIUM 549

CHICKEN AND BARLEY DINNER

Vegetable cooking spray
1 cup diced onion
⅔ cup diced leek
½ teaspoon dried whole thyme
1 cup barley, uncooked
¼ teaspoon salt
⅛ teaspoon pepper
1 (10¾-ounce) can chicken broth, undiluted
¼ cup water
⅔ cup coarsely chopped carrot
6 (4-ounce) boneless chicken breast halves, skinned
3 tablespoons all-purpose flour
2 teaspoons unsalted margarine, melted

Coat a 2½-quart shallow, ovenproof ceramic casserole with cooking spray; place over medium heat until hot. Add onion, and sauté 2 to 3 minutes or until translucent. Add leek and thyme; cook 1 minute, stirring constantly. Stir in barley, salt, pepper, broth, and water; bring to a boil. Remove from heat. Cover; transfer to oven. Bake at 350° for 30 minutes. Add carrot and additional water, if needed. Return to oven; bake 20 to 30 minutes or until barley is tender and liquid is absorbed.

Dredge chicken in flour, and cook in margarine in a nonstick skillet over medium heat 5 to 6 minutes or until golden brown. Spoon barley onto a platter, and top with chicken. Yield: 6 servings (310 calories per serving).

PROTEIN 30.5 / FAT 5.0 / CARBOHYDRATE 34.7 / FIBER 2.9 / CHOLESTEROL 70 / SODIUM 329 / POTASSIUM 418

Arroz con Pollo (page 29), Spanish and Mexican in origin, means "rice with chicken." The rice obtains its golden yellow color from saffron, a spice made from the dried, golden-orange stigmas of an autumn-flowering crocus.

Lemon-Grilled Turkey Breast (page 68) has a distinctive hickory-smoked flavor.

A topping of picante sauce, yogurt, and green chilies adds to the robust flavor of Chicken Fajitas (page 38).

Baby carrots and a rich wine sauce make Cornish Hens with Mushroom-Wine Sauce (page 57) something special.

Chicken-Vegetable Pot Pies (page 7) make a simple-to-prepare supper with down-home flavor.

Southern Stuffed Turkey Breast (page 66) is a flavorful way to enjoy turkey throughout the year.

Poultry, a preferred source of animal protein, never lacks for interest in its presentation. Clockwise from front: Chicken Paillards (page 55), Phyllo Chicken Pot Pie (page 47), and Cold Fruited Chicken (page 6).

Tropical Chicken Kabobs (page 11) combine the fresh flavors of lime, papaya, and pineapple.

Turkey Cutlets with Dijon Pecan Sauce (page 74) makes the ideal entrée for a small dinner party. It's elegant in both appearance and taste but so easy to prepare. Serve it with a green vegetable and a salad, and your main course is complete.

Slice Apple Stuffed Chicken Rolls and arrange them to show off the spiral apple filling (page 25).

CHICKEN WITH SHIITAKE MUSHROOM SAUCE

2 teaspoons chicken-flavored bouillon granules
2 cups water
1 ounce dried shiitake mushrooms (about 1 cup)
2 teaspoons cornstarch
1 tablespoon Madeira or dry sherry
4 (4-ounce) boneless chicken breast halves, skinned
3 tablespoons all-purpose flour
¼ teaspoon pepper
Vegetable cooking spray
2 teaspoons unsalted margarine
¼ cup minced shallots
½ teaspoon dried whole thyme
½ teaspoon peppercorns, crushed
¼ cup dry white wine
1 clove garlic, minced
1 tablespoon minced fresh parsley

Combine bouillon granules and water in a saucepan; bring to a boil. Remove from heat, and add mushrooms. Let stand 30 minutes. Drain, reserving broth. Remove stems from mushrooms, and reserve for other uses; cut caps into fourths, and set aside. Combine cornstarch and Madeira in a small bowl, and set aside.

Place chicken between 2 sheets of waxed paper; flatten to ¼-inch thickness, using a meat mallet or rolling pin. Dredge chicken in flour, and sprinkle with pepper. Coat a large skillet with cooking spray; add margarine, and place over medium heat until margarine melts. Add chicken, and cook 2 to 3 minutes on each side or until lightly browned; transfer to a platter. Add shallots to skillet, and cook 1 minute. Stir in reserved mushrooms, thyme, and crushed peppercorns; cook 3 minutes, tossing gently. Add wine, and cook until mixture is reduced by half. Add reserved mushroom broth and garlic; cover and simmer 10 minutes. Add chicken, and simmer 5 minutes.

Transfer chicken to a serving platter. Cook sauce until reduced to 1¼ cups; stir in cornstarch mixture. Bring to a boil. Cook 1 minute or until sauce is slightly thickened, stirring constantly.

Spoon over chicken; garnish with parsley. Yield: 4 servings (225 calories per serving).

PROTEIN 27.5 / FAT 5.2 / CARBOHYDRATE 14.7 / FIBER 1.2 / CHOLESTEROL 70 / SODIUM 256 / POTASSIUM 394

HERB BAKED CHICKEN

½ cup fine, dry breadcrumbs
¼ cup grated Parmesan cheese
½ teaspoon dried whole oregano
¼ teaspoon dried whole basil
¼ teaspoon pepper
6 (6½-ounce) chicken breast halves, skinned
½ cup buttermilk
Vegetable cooking spray

Combine first 5 ingredients in a shallow dish. Dip chicken in buttermilk, and dredge in breadcrumb mixture. Arrange chicken, bone side down, in a 13- x 9- x 2-inch baking dish coated with cooking spray; cover and refrigerate 1 hour. Bake, uncovered, at 350° for 1 hour, turning after 30 minutes. Yield: 6 servings (201 calories per serving).

PROTEIN 30.2 / FAT 4.7 / CARBOHYDRATE 7.4 / FIBER 0.1 / CHOLESTEROL 78 / SODIUM 210 / POTASSIUM 275

CHICKEN PAILLARDS

4 (4-ounce) boneless chicken breast halves, skinned
2 tablespoons rum
2 tablespoons reduced-sodium soy sauce
3 tablespoons lime juice
1 tablespoon plus 1½ teaspoons brown sugar
1 tablespoon Worcestershire sauce
1 tablespoon vegetable oil
⅛ teaspoon pepper
Vegetable cooking spray
1 tablespoon minced fresh parsley
1 lime, cut into 4 wedges

Place chicken between 2 sheets of waxed paper; flatten to ¼-inch thickness, using a meat mallet or rolling pin: set aside. Combine next 7 ingredients in a shallow dish; mixing well. Add chicken to marinade, turning to coat well; cover and marinate in refrigerator 30 minutes.

Coat a nonstick skillet or ridged grill pan with cooking spray, and place over medium heat until hot. Remove chicken from marinade, and place in skillet; cook 4 minutes on each side or until tender. Transfer chicken to a platter, and garnish with parsley. Squeeze lime over chicken before serving. Yield: 4 servings (193 calories per serving).

PROTEIN 26.4 / FAT 6.4 / CARBOHYDRATE 5.9 / FIBER 0.0 / CHOLESTEROL 70 / SODIUM 390 / POTASSIUM 267

CHICKEN BREAST FRICASSEE

4 (4-ounce) boneless chicken breast halves, skinned
⅛ teaspoon pepper
Vegetable cooking spray
½ pound small white onions
½ pound mushrooms, quartered
½ pound carrots, scraped and diagonally sliced
1 cup frozen whole kernel corn
1 cup water
¼ cup dry white wine
1 teaspoon chicken-flavored bouillon granules
1 teaspoon dried whole tarragon
½ teaspoon dried whole thyme
1 bay leaf
1 tablespoon cornstarch
½ cup evaporated skim milk
1 teaspoon lemon juice
1 sprig fresh tarragon (optional)

Sprinkle chicken with pepper, and set aside. Coat a Dutch oven with cooking spray, and place over medium heat until hot. Add chicken, and cook 2 minutes on each side. Add next 10 ingredients; bring to a boil. Cover; reduce heat, and simmer 15 minutes or until vegetables are tender and chicken is done. Remove chicken to a serving platter, and keep warm.

Dissolve cornstarch in evaporated skim milk; add to Dutch oven, stirring well. Bring to a boil; reduce heat, and simmer until thickened. Remove from heat; stir in lemon juice. Discard bay leaf.

Arrange vegetables around chicken on platter; pour sauce over top, and garnish with fresh tarragon, if desired. Yield: 4 servings (262 calories per serving).

PROTEIN 31.7 / FAT 3.9 / CARBOHYDRATE 26.8 / FIBER 2.3 / CHOLESTEROL 72 / SODIUM 216 / POTASSIUM 856

Cornish Hens

CORNISH HENS WITH MUSHROOM-WINE SAUCE

Vegetable cooking spray
1 teaspoon vegetable oil
½ cup minced green onions
¼ cup minced carrot
1 tablespoon all-purpose flour
¾ cup Chablis or other dry white wine
¾ cup water
½ teaspoon chicken-flavored bouillon granules
½ teaspoon dried whole rosemary
¼ teaspoon dried whole thyme
¼ teaspoon garlic powder
1 bay leaf
½ pound fresh mushrooms, halved
4 (1½-pound) Cornish hens, skinned
1 teaspoon coarsely ground pepper
1 (12-ounce) package baby carrots, scraped
2 stalks celery, cut diagonally into 1-inch pieces
Fresh thyme sprigs (optional)

Coat a large nonstick skillet with cooking spray; add vegetable oil. Place over medium-high heat until hot. Add green onions and carrot; sauté until crisp-tender. Stir in flour. Cook over medium heat 1 minute, stirring constantly. Stir in wine and next 7 ingredients. Bring to a boil. Reduce heat; simmer 5 to 10 minutes, stirring often.

Remove giblets from hens; reserve for other uses. Rinse hens with cold, running water, and pat dry. Split each hen in half lengthwise, using an electric knife. Sprinkle with pepper.

Coat a roasting pan with cooking spray. Place hens, cut side down, in pan. Spoon mushroom sauce over top. Cover and bake at 350° for 45 minutes, basting frequently. Add baby carrots and celery. Cover and bake an additional 20 minutes or until vegetables are crisp-tender and hens are done. Remove and discard bay leaf. Garnish with fresh thyme sprigs, if desired. Yield: 8 servings (240 calories per serving).

PROTEIN 36.3 / FAT 6.1 / CARBOHYDRATE 8.7 / CHOLESTEROL 10 / IRON 2.4 / SODIUM 204 / CALCIUM 46

TANDOORI CORNISH HENS

4 (1-pound, 6-ounce) Cornish hens
½ cup plain nonfat yogurt
½ cup lemon juice
3 cloves garlic
1 tablespoon paprika
1 teaspoon ground cardamom
½ teaspoon ground ginger
½ teaspoon red pepper
Vegetable cooking spray
Fresh cilantro sprigs (optional)

Remove giblets from hens; reserve for other uses. Rinse hens with cold water, and pat dry. Split each hen lengthwise, using an electric knife. Remove and discard skin. Place hens, cavity side up, in a shallow dish.

Combine yogurt and next 6 ingredients in container of an electric blender or food processor; process until smooth. Pour mixture over hens; cover and marinate in refrigerator 8 hours or overnight, turning occasionally.

Arrange hens, cavity side down, on broiler pans coated with cooking spray; brush with yogurt mixture. Broil 6 inches from heating element 7 minutes; turn and broil 5 minutes or until tender. Transfer to a platter, and garnish with cilantro, if desired. Serve immediately. Yield: 8 servings (228 calories per serving).

PROTEIN 33.2 / FAT 8.4 / CARBOHYDRATE 3.6 / CHOLESTEROL 99 / IRON 1.6 / SODIUM 107 / CALCIUM 51

GARLIC-SAGE ROASTED CORNISH HENS

4 (1⅜-pound) Cornish hens, skinned
2 cloves garlic, crushed
¼ teaspoon dried whole sage or 1 teaspoon minced fresh
  sage
2 teaspoons olive oil
⅛ teaspoon coarse salt
Pepper

Remove giblets from hens, and reserve for other uses. Rinse hens with cold water, and pat dry. Lift wingtips up and over back so they are tucked under hen. Close cavities, and tie leg ends together with string; set aside.

Combine garlic and next 3 ingredients; spread on hens. Sprinkle lightly with pepper. Place hens, breast side up, in a shallow roasting pan.

Bake at 350° for 1 hour, basting often with pan drippings. Split hens lengthwise to serve. Yield: 8 servings (222 calories per serving).

PROTEIN 32.1 / FAT 9.3 / CARBOHYDRATE 0.3 / CHOLESTEROL 99 / IRON 1.4 / SODIUM 132 / CALCIUM 19

TROPICAL CORNISH HENS

2 (1-pound) Cornish hens, skinned
½ teaspoon coarsely ground pepper
Vegetable cooking spray
2 tablespoons plus 2 teaspoons frozen orange juice concentrate, thawed and undiluted
1 tablespoon bourbon
⅛ teaspoon garlic powder
1 firm, ripe banana, peeled and coarsely chopped
½ cup peeled, diced fresh mango
½ cup unsweetened pineapple chunks

Orange slices (optional)
Orange curls (optional)

Remove giblets from hens; reserve for other uses. Rinse hens under cold, running water, and pat dry. Split each hen in half lengthwise, using an electric knife. Sprinkle with pepper.

Place hens, cut side down, in a roasting pan that has been coated with cooking spray.

Combine orange juice concentrate, bourbon, and garlic powder in a small bowl. Brush hens with orange juice mixture. Bake at 350° for 45 minutes, basting frequently with orange juice mixture. Add banana, mango, and pineapple to pan. Drizzle with remaining orange juice mixture. Bake 20 minutes or until fruit is thoroughly heated and hens are done. If desired, garnish with orange slices and orange curls. Yield: 4 servings (264 calories per serving).

PROTEIN 27.8 / FAT 7.3 / CARBOHYDRATE 21.2 / CHOLESTEROL 83 / IRON 1.5 / SODIUM 82 / CALCIUM 27

ORIENTAL GRILLED CORNISH HENS

4 (1⅜-pound) Cornish hens
⅔ cup unsweetened pineapple juice
⅓ cup dry sherry
¼ cup reduced-sodium soy sauce
1 tablespoon sesame seeds
1 tablespoon honey
1 clove garlic, minced
⅛ teaspoon ground ginger or 1 teaspoon grated fresh
    gingerroot
Vegetable cooking spray

Remove giblets from hens; reserve for other uses. Rinse hens with cold water, and pat dry. Split each hen lengthwise, using an electric knife. Place hens, cavity side up, in a large shallow dish. Combine next 7 ingredients; pour over hens. Cover and marinate in refrigerator 8 hours or overnight.

Remove hens from marinade, reserving marinade. Coat grill with cooking spray. Grill hens 6 to 7 inches over medium coals 1 hour to 1 hour and 15 minutes or until done, turning hens and basting with marinade every 15 minutes. Yield: 8 servings (256 calories per serving).

PROTEIN 33.1 / FAT 8.8 / CARBOHYDRATE 6.4 / FIBER 0.1 / CHOLESTEROL 99 / SODIUM 388 / POTASSIUM 315

CORNISH HENS VÉRONIQUE

4 (1¼-pound) Cornish hens, skinned
⅛ teaspoon dried whole thyme
⅛ teaspoon pepper
1 tablespoon cornstarch
1 (10¾-ounce) can chicken broth, diluted
1½ cups dry white wine
¾ pound seedless green grapes

Remove giblets from hens; reserve for another use. Rinse hens with cold water; pat dry. Sprinkle with thyme and pepper; arrange in a large roasting pan. Bake at 350° for 1 hour and 15 minutes or until done. Transfer to a platter; keep warm. Transfer pan drippings to a saucepan.

Combine cornstarch and broth in a bowl; set aside. Add wine to saucepan, and cook over high heat until mixture is reduced by half, stirring constantly. Add broth mixture and grapes, and simmer 6 minutes or until thickened.

Press one third of grapes through a sieve, discarding skins; add pulp to sauce, mixing well. Split each hen in half lengthwise, and arrange on individual plates. Spoon sauce over hens. Yield: 8 servings (243 calories per serving with 3 tablespoons sauce per serving).

PROTEIN 30.8 / FAT 8.1 / CARBOHYDRATE 10.6 / FIBER 0.7 / CHOLESTEROL 90 / SODIUM 308 / POTASSIUM 424

CORNISH HENS WITH SPRING VEGETABLES

¾ pound new potatoes, quartered
2 tablespoons lemon juice
1 clove garlic, minced
½ teaspoon pepper
¼ teaspoon dried whole rosemary
¼ teaspoon dried whole thyme
2 (1¼-pound) Cornish hens, skinned
Vegetable cooking spray
1 clove garlic, minced
½ teaspoon pepper
3 cups sliced leeks, cut into 1-inch pieces
1 cup sliced carrots
½ cup sliced green onion
¼ cup dry white wine
¼ cup water
¼ teaspoon salt
¼ pound fresh asparagus, cut into 1-inch pieces

Cook potatoes in boiling water to cover 5 minutes; drain and set aside. Combine lemon juice, 1 clove garlic, ½ teaspoon pepper, rosemary, and thyme in a small bowl. Brush inside and outside of hens with mixture.

Spread next 8 ingredients in a 10- x 6- x 2-inch baking dish coated with cooking spray; top with hens. Cover with aluminum foil; bake at 350° for 45 minutes. Uncover; baste with pan juices. Bake an additional 40 minutes or until done.

Cook asparagus in boiling water in a saucepan 3 to 4 minutes or until crisp-tender; drain. Split each hen in half lengthwise, and arrange on individual plates. Divide asparagus and baked vegetables evenly among plates. Yield: 4 servings (333 calories per serving).

PROTEIN 33.7 / FAT 8.0 / CARBOHYDRATE 32.2 / FIBER 2.8 / CHOLESTEROL 90 / SODIUM 267 / POTASSIUM 1059

Turkey

ROSEMARY TURKEY PATTIES

1 (1-pound) package frozen raw ground turkey, thawed
¼ cup soft whole wheat breadcrumbs
1 egg, slightly beaten
3 tablespoons finely minced onion
2 tablespoons chopped fresh parsley
½ teaspoon salt
½ teaspoon dried whole thyme
¼ teaspoon dried whole rosemary, crushed
Vegetable cooking spray
Rosemary Sauce (recipe follows)
Chopped fresh parsley (optional)

Combine turkey and next 7 ingredients, stirring well. Shape into 6 patties.

Place patties in a 12- x 8- x 2-inch baking dish that has been coated with cooking spray. Bake uncovered, at 350° for 30 to 45 minutes, or until done, turning once. Spoon Rosemary Sauce evenly over patties. Sprinkle with parsley if desired. Yield: 6 servings (149 calories per serving).

Rosemary Sauce:

1 tablespoon margarine
½ cup chopped onion
1 clove garlic, minced
1 tablespoon all-purpose flour
½ teaspoon dried whole rosemary, crushed
½ teaspoon chicken-flavored bouillon granules
¼ cup plus 2 tablespoons water
¼ cup plus 2 tablespoons skim milk

Melt margarine in a small saucepan. Add onion and garlic; sauté until tender. Add flour and rosemary; cook, stirring constantly, 1 minute. Gradually add bouillon granules, water, and skim milk. Cook over medium heat, stirring constantly, until thickened. Yield: ¾ cup.

PROTEIN 18.8 / FAT 5.4 / CARBOHYDRATE 5.3 / CHOLESTEROL 95 / IRON 1.7 / SODIUM 376 / CALCIUM 51

BLUE CHEESE–STUFFED TURKEY BURGERS

1 (1-pound) package frozen raw ground turkey, thawed
1 tablespoon white wine Worcestershire sauce
1 egg, beaten
3 tablespoons crumbled blue cheese
2 tablespoons minced fresh cilantro
Vegetable cooking spray
4 lettuce leaves
2 whole wheat hamburger buns, split and toasted

Combine first 3 ingredients; stir well. Shape turkey mixture into 8 (¼-inch-thick) patties, and set aside.

Combine blue cheese and cilantro. Place 1 tablespoon cheese mixture in center of 4 patties. Top with remaining patties, sealing edges well. Coat grill rack with cooking spray; place on grill over medium-hot coals. Place patties on rack, and cook 6 to 8 minutes on each side or until done.

Place a lettuce leaf and turkey patty on each bun half. Serve immediately. Yield: 4 servings (285 calories per serving).

PROTEIN 31.3 / FAT 10.9 / CARBOHYDRATE 13.7 / CHOLESTEROL 150 / IRON 2.6 / SODIUM 419 / CALCIUM 110

SWEET-AND-SOUR TURKEY MEATBALLS

1 (20-ounce) can unsweetened pineapple chunks,
   undrained
1 (1-pound) package frozen raw ground turkey, thawed
1 egg, lightly beaten
1 cup soft breadcrumbs
½ teaspoon salt
½ teaspoon ground ginger
Vegetable cooking spray
3 green onions, cut into 1-inch pieces
1 large clove garlic, minced
2 teaspoons cornstarch
2 tablespoons cider vinegar
1 tablespoon brown sugar
1 (6-ounce) package frozen snow pea pods, thawed

Drain pineapple chunks, reserving ¼ cup juice; set aside.

Combine ground turkey, egg, breadcrumbs, salt, and ground ginger in a large bowl; stir well. Shape turkey mixture into 1¼-inch meatballs.

Coat a large nonstick skillet with cooking spray; place over medium-high heat until hot. Add meatballs, and cook until lightly browned. Remove meatballs from skillet; set aside and keep warm. Add onions and garlic to skillet, and sauté until tender. Remove from heat.

Combine reserved pineapple juice and cornstarch in a small bowl, stirring until smooth. Add cornstarch mixture, cider vinegar, and brown sugar to skillet. Bring to a boil, stirring constantly. Boil 1 minute or until slightly thickened. Add reserved turkey meatballs, pineapple chunks, and snow peas to skillet. Cook 3 to 5 minutes or until snow peas are crisp-tender. Yield: 6 servings (184 calories per serving).

PROTEIN 19.3 / FAT 3.8 / CARBOHYDRATE 18.0 / CHOLESTEROL 95 / IRON 2.4 / SODIUM 305 / CALCIUM 45

SOUTHERN STUFFED TURKEY BREAST

½ cup cornmeal
¼ cup all-purpose flour
1 teaspoon baking powder
½ teaspoon poultry seasoning
¼ teaspoon baking soda
¼ teaspoon salt
¼ teaspoon rubbed sage
½ cup nonfat buttermilk
1 egg, beaten
Vegetable cooking spray
¼ cup finely chopped celery
3 tablespoons chopped onion
1 (8-ounce) can sliced water chestnuts, drained and
    chopped
1 egg, slightly beaten
¾ teaspoon chicken-flavored bouillon granules
¼ teaspoon pepper
1 (3-pound) boneless turkey breast, skinned
1 tablespoon margarine, melted
1 tablespoon honey
Baby corn (optional)
Fresh sage leaves (optional)
Fresh celery leaves (optional)

Combine first 7 ingredients in a medium bowl; make a well in center of mixture. Combine buttermilk and egg; add to dry ingredients, stirring just until moistened. Spoon cornbread mixture into a preheated 6-inch cast-iron skillet that has been coated with cooking spray. Bake at 400° for 16 to 18 minutes or until browned. Let cool.

Coat a small nonstick skillet with cooking spray; place over medium-high heat until hot. Add celery and onion, and sauté until tender.

Crumble cornbread into a large bowl. Add sautéed celery and onion, water chestnuts, egg, bouillon granules, and pepper; stir well.

Lay turkey breast flat on wax paper, skin side down. Remove tendons, skin, and fat, keeping meat intact. From center, slice horizontally (parallel with skin) through thickest part of each side of breast almost to outer edge; flip cut piece and breast fillets over to enlarge breast. Pound breast to ½-inch thickness.

Spoon stuffing mixture in center of turkey breast, leaving a 2-inch border at sides. Roll up turkey breast over filling, starting from bottom. Tie turkey breast securely at 2-inch intervals with string. Place seam side down on a rack in a shallow roasting pan that has been coated with cooking spray. Insert meat thermometer. Bake, covered, at 325° for 30 minutes.

Combine margarine and honey; brush over turkey. Bake, uncovered, 1½ hours or until meat thermometer registers 185°. Transfer turkey to a cutting board; remove string. Let stand 10 minutes before slicing. If desired, garnish with baby corn and fresh sage and celery leaves. Yield: 10 servings (210 calories per serving).

PROTEIN 29.9 / FAT 3.4 / CARBOHYDRATE 13.1 / CHOLESTEROL 130 / IRON 2.0 / SODIUM 274 / CALCIUM 46

TURKEY LOAF WITH MUSTARD SAUCE

2 (1-pound) packages raw ground turkey, thawed
2 cups soft whole wheat breadcrumbs
½ cup shredded carrot
¼ cup finely chopped onion
2 eggs, beaten
1 tablespoon minced fresh parsley
1½ teaspoons dry mustard
½ teaspoon pepper
Vegetable cooking spray
Fresh dill sprigs (optional)
Mustard Sauce (recipe follows)

Combine first 8 ingredients in a large bowl; stir well. Place mixture on a broiler rack coated with cooking spray, and shape into a slightly rounded loaf. (Mixture will be soft.) Bake at 350° for 1 hour and 10 minutes or until meat is no longer pink. Transfer loaf to a serving platter, and garnish with dill sprigs, if desired. Serve with 2 tablespoons Mustard Sauce per serving. Yield: 10 servings (229 calories per serving).

Mustard Sauce:

1 cup reduced-calorie mayonnaise
3 tablespoons water
2 tablespoons lemon juice
1 tablespoon plus 1 teaspoon Dijon mustard
1 teaspoon dried whole dillweed

Combine all ingredients in a small saucepan, stirring well. Cook over low heat, stirring constantly, 2 minutes or until thoroughly heated. Yield: 1⅓ cups.

PROTEIN 22.7 / FAT 11.5 / CARBOHYDRATE 7.9 / CHOLESTEROL 115 / IRON 1.8 / SODIUM 354 / CALCIUM 39

LEMON-GRILLED TURKEY BREAST

¼ cup lemon juice
2 tablespoons vegetable oil
2 cloves garlic, crushed
1 teaspoon dried whole dillweed
½ teaspoon grated lemon rind
½ teaspoon paprika
½ teaspoon pepper
1 (4-pound) boneless turkey breast, skinned
Hickory chips
Vegetable cooking spray

Combine first 7 ingredients in a small bowl, stirring well. Set aside.

Rinse turkey with cold water, and pat dry. Roll turkey loosely, securing any loose pieces with string. Brush turkey with half of reserved lemon juice mixture. Set aside remaining lemon juice mixture.

Prepare charcoal fire in commercial meat smoker; let fire burn 15 to 20 minutes. Soak hickory chips in water 15 minutes, and place chips on coals. Place water pan in smoker; fill pan with water.

Place turkey on rack coated with cooking spray. Insert meat thermometer, if desired. Cover with smoker lid; cook 8 hours or until meat thermometer registers 185°, basting turkey with remaining lemon juice mixture after 4 hours. Refill water pan with water, and add additional charcoal as needed.

Transfer turkey breast to a cutting board; remove string. Slice turkey. Transfer turkey slices to a serving platter. Yield: 14 servings (156 calories per serving).

PROTEIN 25.9 / FAT 4.8 / CARBOHYDRATE 0.7 / CHOLESTEROL 60 / IRON 1.3 / SODIUM 56 / CALCIUM 19

TURKEY YAKI TORI

½ cup rice wine
¼ cup Sauterne
2 tablespoons firmly packed brown sugar
2 tablespoons reduced-sodium soy sauce
1 pound boneless turkey breast, skinned
1 small green pepper, seeded and cut into 1-inch pieces
4 green onions with tops, cut into 1-inch pieces

Combine first 4 ingredients in a saucepan. Bring to a boil; reduce heat, and simmer, uncovered, 5 minutes. Remove from heat; let cool.

Rinse turkey with cold water, and pat dry. Cut into 1-inch cubes. Place cubes in a shallow container. Pour cooled marinade over turkey. Cover; refrigerate 8 hours or overnight.

Drain turkey, reserving marinade. Alternate turkey cubes, green pepper, and green onions on four 12-inch wooden skewers. Grill 5 to 6 inches from hot coals 10 to 12 minutes or until desired degree of doneness. Turn and brush turkey and vegetables frequently with reserved marinade. Yield: 4 servings (173 calories per serving).

PROTEIN 23.6 / FAT 2.6 / CARBOHYDRATE 12.5 / CHOLESTEROL 52 / IRON 1.7 / SODIUM 345 / CALCIUM 33

TURKEY HASH

Vegetable cooking spray
⅔ cup sliced fresh mushrooms
2 tablespoons chopped onion
2 tablespoons chopped green pepper
2 tablespoons chopped sweet red pepper
3 tablespoons margarine
¼ cup plus 1 tablespoon all-purpose flour
1½ teaspoons chicken-flavored bouillon granules
1½ cups skim milk
1½ cups water
½ teaspoon pepper
¼ teaspoon paprika
5 cups chopped, cooked turkey breast (skinned before cooking and cooked without salt)
Fresh parsley sprigs

Coat a large skillet with cooking spray. Place over medium heat until hot. Add mushrooms, onion, green pepper, and sweet red pepper; cook until vegetables are tender. Remove vegetables from skillet, and set aside.

Melt margarine in skillet over low heat. Add flour and bouillon granules, stirring until smooth. Cook 1 minute, stirring constantly (mixture will be dry). Gradually add skim milk and water; cook over medium heat, stirring constantly with a wire whisk, until smooth and thickened. Stir in pepper, paprika, turkey, and reserved vegetables. Cook until thoroughly heated. Garnish with parsley sprigs. Yield: 8 servings (216 calories per serving).

PROTEIN 28.4 / FAT 7.4 / CARBOHYDRATE 7.3 / CHOLESTEROL 61 / IRON 1.6 / SODIUM 202 / CALCIUM 78

ORANGE-BAKED TURKEY

1 (4½-pound) turkey breast, skinned
2 cups water
1 cup unsweetened orange juice
2 teaspoons chicken-flavored bouillon granules
1 tablespoon cornstarch
3 tablespoons Cointreau or other orange-flavored liqueur
1 tablespoon grated orange rind
1½ cups unsweetened orange juice
¼ teaspoon pepper
Fresh parsley sprigs
Orange slices

Place turkey breast in a large roasting pan. Combine 2 cups water, 1 cup orange juice, and bouillon granules, stirring until granules dissolve; pour over turkey. Insert meat thermometer into meaty portion of breast, if desired, making sure it does not touch bone. Cover and bake at 325° for 3 hours or until meat thermometer registers 185°, basting frequently.

Combine cornstarch, Cointreau, orange rind, 1½ cups orange juice, and pepper in a nonaluminum saucepan; stir until smooth. Cook over medium heat, stirring constantly, until thickened and bubbly.

Slice turkey; transfer to a large platter. Garnish with parsley and orange slices. Serve with 1 tablespoon orange sauce per serving. Yield: 12 servings (177 calories per serving).

PROTEIN 28.4 / FAT 3.1 / CARBOHYDRATE 5.2 / FIBER 0.0 / CHOLESTEROL 65 / SODIUM 61 / POTASSIUM 350

SPICY TURKEY PATTIES

1 (1-pound) package raw ground turkey, thawed
¼ cup soft breadcrumbs
1 egg, beaten
1 tablespoon dried onion flakes
1 clove garlic, minced
1 tablespoon Worcestershire sauce
1 teaspoon prepared mustard
½ teaspoon chili powder
¼ teaspoon pepper
⅛ teaspoon hot sauce
Vegetable cooking spray
Pepper-Onion Sauce (recipe follows)

Combine first 10 ingredients in a bowl; stir well. Shape mixture into 4 (¾-inch-thick) patties. Place patties on rack of a broiler pan coated with cooking spray; broil 5 inches from heating element 5 minutes on each side or until desired degree of doneness. Serve with 2 tablespoons sauce per serving. Yield: 4 servings (199 calories per serving).

Pepper-Onion Sauce:

Vegetable cooking spray
3 tablespoons finely chopped green pepper
3 tablespoons finely chopped onion
⅓ cup reduced-calorie catsup
½ teaspoon firmly packed brown sugar
¼ teaspoon horseradish

Coat a small skillet with cooking spray; place over medium heat until hot. Add green pepper and onion, and sauté 3 minutes or until tender. Add remaining ingredients; cook, stirring constantly, until thoroughly heated. Serve warm or chilled. Yield: ½ cup.

PROTEIN 27.3 / FAT 5.0 / CARBOHYDRATE 8.8 / FIBER 0.6 / CHOLESTEROL 142 / SODIUM 194 / POTASSIUM 603

TURKEY STIR-FRY

1 pound turkey breast cutlets
¼ cup dry sherry
2 tablespoons reduced-sodium soy sauce
2 tablespoons water
1 teaspoon firmly packed brown sugar
Vegetable cooking spray
1 tablespoon vegetable oil
1 clove garlic, minced
1 cup broccoli flowerets
1 medium onion, thinly sliced
2 medium carrots, scraped and cut diagonally into ½-inch
   slices
1 cup sliced fresh mushrooms
1 medium-size sweet red pepper, seeded and cut into
   ¼-inch strips
2 teaspoons cornstarch
2 cups hot cooked brown rice (cooked without salt or fat)

Cut turkey across the grain into 3- x ½-inch strips; place in a
shallow container, and set aside. Combine sherry, soy sauce,
water, and brown sugar; mix well. Pour over turkey, tossing to
coat. Cover and refrigerate 30 minutes.

Coat a wok with cooking spray. Pour vegetable oil around top of
wok; heat at medium-high (325°) for 2 minutes. Add garlic; stir-fry
1 minute. Drain turkey, reserving marinade. Add turkey strips to
wok; stir-fry 2 minutes. Add broccoli, onion, and carrots; stir-fry
2 minutes. Add mushrooms and red pepper; stir-fry 2 minutes.

Add cornstarch to reserved marinade, stirring well. Pour over
turkey mixture. Cook, stirring constantly, 2 minutes or until
slightly thickened. Serve hot over brown rice. Yield: 4 servings
(240 calories per serving plus 102 calories per ½ cup cooked rice).

PROTEIN 30.9 / FAT 7.1 / CARBOHYDRATE 33.4 / FIBER 3.2 / CHOLESTEROL 61 / SODIUM 365 /
POTASSIUM 633

TURKEY CUTLETS WITH DIJON PECAN SAUCE

8 (2-ounce) turkey breast cutlets
¼ cup all-purpose flour
⅛ teaspoon pepper
Vegetable cooking spray
1 tablespoon margarine
½ cup dry white wine
½ cup water
2 tablespoons Dijon mustard
2 teaspoons honey
½ teaspoon chicken-flavored bouillon granules
2 tablespoons chopped, toasted pecans
Fresh parsley sprigs

Place each turkey cutlet between 2 sheets of waxed paper; flatten to ¼-inch thickness, using a meat mallet or rolling pin. Combine flour and pepper; dredge cutlets in flour mixture.

Coat a large skillet with cooking spray; add margarine, and place over medium heat until margarine melts. Add cutlets, and cook 3 to 4 minutes on each side or until golden brown. Remove turkey, and drain on paper towels; transfer to a platter, and keep warm.

Wipe skillet dry with a paper towel. Combine wine, water, mustard, honey, and bouillon granules in skillet; cook, uncovered, 10 minutes or until liquid is reduced to ½ cup, stirring occasionally. Stir in pecans, and spoon evenly over cutlets. Garnish with parsley. Yield: 4 servings (246 calories per serving).

PROTEIN 27.7 / FAT 8.9 / CARBOHYDRATE 11.9 / FIBER 0.3 / CHOLESTEROL 61 / SODIUM 364 / POTASSIUM 333

SPINACH-STUFFED TURKEY BREAST

Vegetable cooking spray
1 medium onion, finely chopped
½ cup chopped fresh mushrooms
1 clove garlic, minced
1 (10-ounce) package frozen chopped spinach
1 cup soft whole wheat breadcrumbs
2 tablespoons grated Parmesan cheese
1 egg, beaten
½ teaspoon dried whole thyme
½ teaspoon pepper
1 (3½-pound) boneless turkey breast
¾ teaspoon rubbed sage
¼ teaspoon salt
¼ teaspoon white pepper
¼ teaspoon paprika
Fresh thyme sprigs

Coat a small skillet with cooking spray; place over medium-high heat until hot. Add onion, mushrooms, and garlic to skillet; sauté until tender, and set aside.

Cook spinach according to package directions, omitting salt. Drain well, and place on paper towels; squeeze until barely moist. Combine spinach, reserved vegetables, breadcrumbs, Parmesan cheese, egg, thyme, and ½ teaspoon pepper in a small bowl; stir until well blended. Set mixture aside.

Lay turkey breast flat, skin side up, on waxed paper. Carefully slice away tendons, skin, and excess fat, keeping meat intact. Turn turkey breast over carefully to keep center of turkey breast attached. Beginning at center of turkey breast, slice horizontally through thickest part of each side of breast almost to outer edge; flip the cut pieces of breast fillets over and out to enlarge breast surface area and to make a more even thickness. To fill in shallow area between breast halves, slice meat horizontally from thickest parts of breast, and lay slices in shallow area. Pound breast to ½-inch thickness.

Spread reserved spinach mixture over turkey breast, leaving a

½-inch border at sides. Roll up turkey, jelly roll fashion, starting at long side. Sew up seams, using a needle and thread, or secure with wooden picks, if necessary.

Combine sage, salt, white pepper, and paprika in a small bowl; stir well, and rub over outer surface of turkey.

Insert meat thermometer into turkey breast, making sure end touches meat. Place in a browning bag prepared according to package directions. Place in a shallow roasting pan. Bake at 350° for 1 hour or until meat thermometer registers 185°. Transfer to a serving platter; let stand 15 minutes. Remove thread or wooden picks. Slice with an electric knife. Garnish with thyme sprigs before serving. Yield: 10 servings (194 calories per serving).

PROTEIN 30.5 / FAT 4.3 / CARBOHYDRATE 7.5 / FIBER 1.3 / CHOLESTEROL 91 / SODIUM 217 / POTASSIUM 445

LIME TURKEY CUTLETS

⅓ cup all-purpose flour
½ teaspoon pepper
16 (2-ounce) turkey breast cutlets
Vegetable cooking spray
3 tablespoons margarine
½ cup water
½ teaspoon chicken-flavored bouillon granules
3 tablespoons lime juice
¼ teaspoon dried whole dillweed
1 tablespoon chopped parsley
Lime slices

Combine flour and pepper in a small bowl; dredge turkey lightly in flour mixture.

Coat a large nonaluminum skillet with cooking spray; add margarine, and place over medium heat until margarine melts. Add turkey, and cook 2 to 3 minutes on each side or until browned. Remove from skillet, and drain on paper towels. Wipe skillet dry with paper towels.

Combine the water, bouillon granules, lime juice, and dillweed in skillet; add turkey. Cover; simmer over low heat 10 minutes or until turkey is tender. Remove to a warm platter. Sprinkle with parsley, and garnish with lime slices. Yield: 8 servings (195 calories per serving).

PROTEIN 26.1 / FAT 7.2 / CARBOHYDRATE 5.0 / FIBER 0.2 / CHOLESTEROL 59 / SODIUM 131 / POTASSIUM 278

QUICK TURKEY MARSALA

2 (4-ounce) turkey breast slices
Vegetable cooking spray
1 tablespoon unsalted margarine
6 fresh mushrooms, sliced
½ cup Marsala wine
¼ teaspoon salt
Dash of pepper
1 teaspoon lemon juice
2 teaspoons chopped fresh parsley

Place each slice of turkey breast between 2 sheets of waxed paper, and flatten to ¼-inch thickness, using a meat mallet or rolling pin. Set turkey aside.

Coat a medium skillet with cooking spray, and add margarine; place over medium heat until margarine melts. Add turkey, and cook over low heat 4 minutes on each side. Remove turkey to a serving platter, and keep warm. Add mushrooms, wine, salt, pepper, and lemon juice to skillet; cook until mushrooms are tender. Pour wine mixture over turkey, and sprinkle with chopped parsley. Yield: 2 servings (216 calories per serving).

Note: ½ cup white wine plus 2 teaspoons brandy may be substituted for the Marsala wine.

PROTEIN 26.7 / FAT 8.6 / CARBOHYDRATE 7.4 / FIBER 0.4 / CHOLESTEROL 59 / SODIUM 353 / POTASSIUM 514

ROAST TURKEY WITH ZUCCHINI-RICE STUFFING

2 cups cooked brown rice (cooked without fat or salt)
1 medium zucchini, diced
½ cup sliced fresh mushrooms
¼ cup chopped onion
1 egg
½ teaspoon dried whole sage
1 (5-pound) turkey breast, skinned and boned
½ cup water
½ teaspoon chicken-flavored bouillon granules

Combine first 6 ingredients in a bowl, and mix well. Stuff turkey breast cavity with rice mixture, and secure with string; insert meat thermometer, if desired. Place turkey in a browning bag. Pour the water over turkey, and sprinkle with bouillon granules. Bake at 325° for 2 hours or until a meat thermometer registers 185°. Yield: 14 servings (174 calories per serving).

PROTEIN 28.0 / FAT 3.5 / CARBOHYDRATE 5.9 / FIBER 0.6 / CHOLESTEROL 81 / SODIUM 135 / POTASSIUM 328

INDEX

zucchini-rice stuffing with roast turkey, 78

Wild rice and chicken casserole, 34
Wine
  chicken Chablis, 32
  chicken livers in, 31

-mushroom sauce, 57–58
turkey Marsala, quick, 77

Yogurt
  gravy, 30–31
  -marinated chicken, 39

Zucchini-rice stuffing with roast turkey, 78